A Farley Mowat Reader

A Farley Mowat Reader

Edited by Wendy Thomas

Illustrated by Richard Row

Roberts Rinehart Publishers

Copyright © 1997 by Farley Mowat

International Standard Book Number 1-57098-175-2

Library of Congress Catalog Card Number 97-68060

Published by Roberts Rinehart Publishers
6309 Monarch Park Place, Niwot, Colorado 80503
Tel (303) 530.4400 Fax (303) 530.4488

Distributed to the trade in the U.S. by Publishers Group West

10 9 8 7 6 5 4 3 2 1

Contents

Preface by Wendy Thomas

I came to Farley Mowat's writing late in life. I'm not sure how I missed out on reading him when I was younger, but I'm not altogether sorry I did. There's something exciting about "discovering" a "new" writer and finding that he or she has already written enough books to keep you satisfied for months!

This collection of stories is the perfect introduction to ensure that you don't miss out as I did. The best part is that there's lots more where these came from. There are more stories about Mutt (*The Dog Who Wouldn't Be*) and Wol and Weeps (*Owls in the Family*). There's more about the wolf family (*Never Cry Wolf*) and the fate of the whale (*A Whale for the Killing*). And there's more about Mowat's own family, not only in *The Dog Who Wouldn't Be* and *Owls in the Family*, but in his autobiography, *Born Naked*, which with humor and frankness recounts the early years that formed the foundation for the writer, naturalist, and activist he became.

Choosing stories for any collection is challenging. The stories that follow have been selected for several reasons, one of the most important being that each appeals to a part of me that remains rather childish. Each story had to be a "good read"—but so much of Mowat is that, that I then had to put on my editor's hat. I looked for the stories that helped show how Mowat's sensibilities and interests were formed and that showed him in the landscapes and against the backdrops with which he is associated: the prairies, the north, Newfoundland and the sea, and Europe of the Second World War.

After a period of reading, sifting, and with great regret setting some pieces aside in a "maybe not" pile, I came up with a "definitely must have" pile. Alas, it was still too large. But as I continued to edit and assess the DMH pile, themes seemed to assert themselves, which explains the grouping of the stories in this book. Writers' early lives are fascinating to their readers. We like to see the world they grew up in, who their parents and grandparents were, and perhaps we want to see how their youthful dreams and interests mirror our own. We also want to be entertained, and Mowat is never more entertaining than when he is writing about Mutt, whose vivid personality combines the most intriguing canine and human characteristics.

Two important themes in Mowat's writing are his great love for the animal world, evident from his early childhood, and his love for the sea. This was a love he shared with his father, whose spirit of adventure and individuality shines wherever he appears in these pages. It's clear that his son inherited that spirit and even enlarged on it when he decided to take to the seas with his friend Jack McClelland, with whom he had some nautical misadventures, a small part of which is recounted here.

Finally, a thread appeared that ties all these interests together, and that thread traced the making of a writer. Once again, his father offers support and encouragement as Mowat prepares for his life's work.

I chose pieces that did not need much explanation to set the scene. In some cases, the scene was set by Mowat himself, but some pages away from the part of the story I was using. In these situations, I deleted the intervening material but, for ease of reading, did not indicate these deletions by using ellipses (the series of periods conventionally used to show missing material).

There's not room here to list all the Mowat writing that didn't make it into this collection, but a few should be noted. I have not included extracts from any of the fiction Mowat has written for young people, but I urge you to get your hands on *Lost in the Barrens, The Black Joke, The Curse of the Viking Grave,* and *The Snow Walker*—I wanted to leave a few gems for you to uncover yourself.

The works for which Mowat became well-known early on in his career, *People of the Deer* and *The Desperate People,* are also not represented here, nor is *And No Birds Sang,* in which he writes about the horrors of war. The writing in these books is denser and the topics more somber than seemed fitting for this anthology.

Canadian heroes, especially those who are not athletes, are few and far between, but Farley Mowat is one who has stood the test of time. He's funny, irreverent, passionate, and insightful. I hope you have as much fun reading this book and discovering his world as I did putting it together.

Wendy Thomas
Toronto, 1997

Foreword by Farley Mowat

When I was your age I didn't exactly drool with delight if someone gave me a book entitled *The Something-or-Other Reader*. Frankly, it put me off. It sounded too much like work—like schoolwork of the kind my teachers thought was good for me. However, a book was something I couldn't really resist, so I used to paste tape over that awful word "Reader;" and then I could enjoy with a clear conscience. If it had been me, I'd have called this book *Farley's Follies*.

Whether *your* conscience is clear or not, I hope you'll like the book, by whatever title. I have to tell you that I, at any rate, enormously enjoyed writing the stories you'll find here. I enjoyed living most of them, too; although, to tell the truth, there were a few incidents I could have done without.

I had fun poking about in Wendy Thomas's selections from my writings (especially after I got rid of that "Reader" bit), because it was like rummaging about in an old trunk stuffed full of pages from my own life. Lots of memories of good times; fun times; some bad times; scary times; terrific people; and even more terrific animals. It's been an amazing experience because (and this is a secret just between the two of us) my memory is leakier than my old boat used to be. So if I hadn't written down what happened, it would have been gone into the mists forever. I *hope* I didn't hear someone mutter, "Well, that might not have been much of a loss."

I hope, too, that these pages will give you some pleasure. Because, in my opinion, that's what writing is really all about—pleasuring someone just like you.

Farley Mowat
Cape Breton Island, 1997

The Family
Mowat

Beginnings

The world into which I was born in 1921 had not long emerged from a terrible war which devastated much of Europe and slaughtered ten million people. Canada's contribution to that holocaust included eighty thousand soldiers, seamen, and aviators blown to bits, choked with poison gas, drowned in the gray Atlantic, or otherwise obliterated, together with two hundred thousand disabled "veterans," my father amongst them, who came home bearing visible and invisible wounds which would afflict them to the end of their days.

Apart from these unfortunates, the War to End All Wars left Canada and most Canadians in fine fettle. Trenton, a small market town in south-central Ontario, was a case in point. When the war began, Trenton had a population of about a thousand people, mostly of Scots, Irish, and English ancestry, clumped around a fine natural harbor where the mouth of the Trent River empties into the Bay of Quinte. The townsfolk mostly made their livings from quiet trade with the farms which ran northward from the bay shore until the good soil petered out in pine forests and hard-rock country.

The war changed that. Between 1914 and 1918 Trenton was transformed. A military seaplane base mushroomed a few miles to the east; the population swelled and the town feverishly engaged in war production.

The showpiece of this industrial transformation was a vast chemical plant devoted to the manufacture of high explosives. In the words of a local Captain of Commerce: "This progressive industry put Trenton square on the map of the Modern World at last."

And almost wiped it off again when, during the final months of the war, the plant caught fire and blew up. Fortunately it was distant enough so that Trenton escaped being flattened.

Angus Mowat was born in Trenton twenty-six years before the big explosion. His father, Robert McGill Mowat (called Gill), was the son of a professor of exegesis at Queen's University and a nephew of Sir Oliver Mowat, a Kingston lawyer who became premier of Ontario and one of the Fathers of Canadian Confederation. Because of these high connections, it was predicted that Gill would "go far" in the Church or at the Bar.

But Gill was a soft-centered sort of chap who loved snowshoeing, sailing, writing poetry, and contemplating Nature, and was singularly lacking in what was then called "get up and go." However, he *was* good-looking so he married well—to the daughter of an affluent Brockville furniture manufacturer.

When I knew my grandmother Mary Mowat, née Jones, she was a tight-lipped, disappointed woman with a jaundiced view of life. Doubtless she had reason to be sour. When her husband failed to achieve even the minimum requirements for a pastor's post, and his Uncle Oliver's firm tried but failed to make something of him as a lawyer, he was brought into the Jones family business. Here he made such a hash of things that the young couple was banished to sleepy little Trenton at a discreet distance from Kingston and Brockville both.

Gill was established as proprietor of a Trenton hardware store, where he soon demonstrated that he was no more adept at commerce than at the professions or in industry. Kindly to a fault, he gave credit (and cash too) to all who asked. He also tended to be so distracted by his poetic visions as to become a threat to the general public. On one occasion, he absent-mindedly filled an order for a dozen beeswax candles with a dozen sticks of dynamite.

It was perhaps inevitable that the store would fail, but not that it would fail three times. The Mowat and Jones families bailed Gill out twice, then gave up. So he retired in his early fifties, a remittance man living on the income from his wife's inheritance.

I remember him as a slightly absent old chap with a long white mustache yellowed by the smoke from his calabash pipe. He spent a lot of time sitting in an old leather chair staring into space through rheumy blue eyes that, very occasionally, would focus on me. He always seemed surprised to find me standing by his chair, probably because his imagination was far distant, keeping company with Hiawathan braves and dusky maidens. He could have found little enough solace in his own domestic milieu, where he endured a terrible truce dictated by the iron disapproval of an embittered wife.

Apart from having to deal somehow with the stigma of his father's failures, Angus seems to have led a near-idyllic childhood. Small, lean, and wiry, he was a water rat, at home on the mashes (marshes), criks (creeks), swamps, rivers, and lakes where he became a passionate sailor of canoes, punts, dinghies, and anything else that could be made to float.

An indifferent scholar, he nevertheless passed his university entrance examinations in 1913 when he was twenty-one. He spent that summer roaming the forests of Temagami in northern Ontario as an apprentice fire ranger and in the autumn enrolled in the faculty of engineering at Queen's University in Kingston.

In 1914 the Great War began, and Angus enlisted in the army. Within a few months, he had become a participant in the blood-bath that was overwhelming France. Early in 1918, German machine-gun fire shattered his right arm and he was invalided back to Canada. When he was released from hospital, he headed west for Port Arthur, at the head of Lake Superior, in hot pursuit of the woman who would become my mother.

Helen Thomson was the youngest daughter of Henry (Hal) Thomson, who had been manager of the Molson's Bank branch in Trenton until he made some injudicious loans. After the borrowers defaulted, Hal—his career in ruins—was exiled by his employers to Port Arthur, which was the Ontario equivalent of Siberia.

During the last years before the war, Angus had been a determined suitor (one of many) of sloe-eyed, black-haired Helen. But her parents could see no future for her with the son of Gill Mowat and Helen herself was not much taken with Angus, whom she remembered as being a "very pushy little fellow." She fell in love with a young artillery lieutenant who survived the fighting only to die during the great influenza epidemic at war's end.

In the fall of 1918 Angus appeared at the Thomson home in Port Arthur. He looked exceedingly dashing in his officer's uniform, his chest covered with medals and his right arm in a sling. As a returning hero he was now much admired. Although there had been no improvement in *his* prospects, the fortunes of the Thomson family were in such decline that the elder Thomsons could hardly offer much resistance when Angus pressed his suit on Helen. Sad and lonely, in the spring of 1919 she softened and agreed to marry him.

Their wedding picture shows him in dress uniform looking very much the dashing military man. Helen looks lovely, although there is something about her which presages uncertainty. Under the faded photograph is written in an unknown hand (not hers) the piquant query: "Whither away?"

Whither indeed. Their first destination was a log cabin at romantically named Orient Bay north of Lake Superior where Angus again found work as a fire ranger. The newlyweds spent the summer "roughing it in the bush" in company with lumberjacks, black-flies, Indians, black bears, and mosquitoes.

Although, as a wounded veteran, Angus was entitled to special consideration in government employment, his useless arm proved more of a disability than the ranger service could tolerate. In the autumn of 1919, the couple traveled south to the city of Toronto, where a job had been found for Angus as a clerk in a wholesale grocery firm owned by members of his mother's family.

This was not his cup of tea. Incarcerated in a rooming house by night and a counting house by day, he worked from eight until five pushing a pen and counting things. Whether he cared to admit it or not, he was his father's son, and this was a life for which he had neither aptitude nor appetite.

After a month or two he could no longer stand it, but his mother insisted he should stay. The Firm would look after him, she said. All he had to do was be diligent and in due course he would rise. That was the point. One was supposed to make *sure* of one's future. And with his own father's fate to remember, and the knowledge that jobs for cripples were hard to come by, he felt he had to try to stick it out.

He tried. And failed. After a year of servitude, he let it be known that "the doctors" (nameless) had decreed that, for his health's sake, he must find outdoor work. Everyone seems to have believed him, and it may even have been something more than an inspired invention.

Free at last, Angus went right back to his roots. Having packed Helen off to visit her parents for a while (by this time she was pregnant with me), he set off in the autumn of 1920 for Trenton in search of a way of life which would permit him to live according to his own choosing.

Eventually he concluded that his future lay in bee keeping. This was a decision in which Helen had no part. In truth she seldom had any significant say in major family decisions then or later. She was generally phlegmatic about this, although she once ruefully told me that being married to a man who always knew precisely what was best for all of us could be trying. Indeed, Angus was always very much the captain of his own ship and, if he was not infallible, at least he thought he was.

After buying the bees and spending most of his remaining money on a second-hand Model T Ford truck (inevitably named Henry), my father went house hunting.

The post-war boom, which everyone assumed would last forever, was then in full swing. Every enterprise in Trenton from the cooperage mill to the Chinese laundry was doing about as much business as it could handle. Everything was hustle and bustle, which meant there were few houses for sale or rent, and those which were available were beyond Angus's means. In some desperation he took his troubles to Billy Fraser, the town tycoon and owner of the cooperage. Billy had at his disposal an enormous frame house of Gothic architecture, turreted and towered, which had been built by one of the lumber barons of the previous century. Now it stood untenanted, its paint peeling, its massive central tower gaping open to the weather, and its shingles falling away like scales from a scrofulous old dragon.

Billy let Angus and Helen live here by grace-and-favor, as it were, and he let Angus cart away truck loads of hardwood scrap from the cooperage to keep them warm. Nothing short of a volcano could have properly heated that old pile but, by shutting themselves into the winter kitchen and two of the servants' rooms, they at least had a roof over their heads and walls tight enough to keep the water from freezing in the buckets most winter nights.

This was Helen's first home of her own and on May 12, 1921, it became almost but not quite my natal place. As Angus described the event: "From his earliest years Farley had some disregard for the conventions. In the first instance he tried to get out when his mother was in the taxi cab on the way to the hospital, which was ten miles away in Belleville. He nearly did, too. Then, in the hospital, he'd be damned if he'd wait for the doctor, who was something of a slowpoke, so out he popped all over everything. The nurse said that the first thing she knew there he was. She said he rolled over, propped himself up on one elbow and gave her a kind of leer."

Angus was delighted to have a son, but not as delighted as he might have been.

"I much wanted a son who would become a salt-water sailor, perhaps a deep-sea captain," he complained. "Well, Neptune puts his mark on those fated to go down to the sea in ships. They are born with a caul over their heads. This is Neptune's guarantee that they will never drown or, if they do, that they will become Mermen and enjoy a rollicking hereafter among the Mermaids."

Alas, I had not even the vestige of a caul. I came into the world just like every other landlubber does—stark naked.

We remained in Billy Fraser's rambling old ruin through my earliest years, leading a relatively uneventful life but one which was not without its moments. I was painfully slow at learning to use the pot until a night in my second year when all the ceiling plaster in my room fell down on top of me. I used the pot diligently thereafter, fearing that the entire roof would fall in if I didn't.

Our diet consisted mainly of porridge, soda biscuits, and honey. Helen relied heavily on oatmeal. Being a bank manager's daughter, she had been raised

to be a lady. Four years in a convent school had taught her embroidery, how to paint with water-colors, how to declaim poetry, and how to sing in a choir. Nobody had ever taught her culinary skills, but she did learn how to cook oatmeal porridge during her summer with Angus at Orient Bay.

To celebrate our first Christmas together, she reached for the stars and determined to bake a batch of mince pies. All might have gone well had she not asked the butcher for five pounds of mincemeat "and do please cut it from a nice tender young mince."

The bewildered butcher gave her five pounds of bloody, minced (ground) beefsteak, to which she happily added all the other ingredients called for in her cookbook. The resultant pies might have been hailed as *nouveau cuisine tortière* in our time, but not in Trenton in 1921. The neighbor's dog got them and a chastened Helen returned to variations on the theme of oatmeal porridge.

Angus's bees did well at first, producing quantities of good clover and buckwheat honey, but since the market was flooded, the crop could not be sold and we had to consume much of it ourselves. I was weaned on soda biscuits soaked in milk and lavishly sweetened with honey—a dish I still find delectable.

Bees loomed large in my early years. When Angus rattled off in Henry of a summer morning to work his hives in the apple orchard of the Ketcheson farm on York Road, he would often take Helen and me along. Helen would sit under a tree and read. To keep me from crawling into trouble, she would place me in an empty super* set on the grass nearby. This was the scene of my earliest recollection.

I see, in my mind's eye, a large and strikingly marked honey bee standing on an anthill near where I sit. This bee is resolutely and briskly directing the ant traffic away from me, much as a policeman might direct members of an unruly crowd away from some important personage.

I have since been told by expert apiarists that such behavior by a bee would be "atypical," which is a polite way of saying my memory lies. Nonsense. I *know* I was taken under the protection of the bees, and the proof is that I have never been stung by one, not then or ever. Wasps and hornets, yes. Bees, no. I believe I was adopted into their tribe, and ever since I have been as kindly disposed to them as they to me.

A Note About Names

Angus had a mania for naming things, even when they already had perfectly good names. As a freshman mining engineer at Queen's he had re-christened himself Squib. In mining terminology, a squib was a small but potent charge used to detonate a major explosion and this may well have been how he viewed himself.

He was not satisfied with my name either. I had been christened Farley in memory of Helen's beloved younger brother killed in a fall from a cliff, but before I was three months old Angus had begun calling me Bunje after some character he had encountered in a novel by, I think, H. G. Wells. When my mother tearfully remonstrated with him, he airily replied that Bunje was merely my "working title" to be used until I could make up my own mind what I wanted to be called.

---

* A rectangular wooden frame used in the upper portion of a hive.

Angus and Boats

During the summer of 1923 the apiary, which had always been a losing proposition (we kept bees . . . not vice versa), was smitten by a pestilence called "foul brood." The bees perished in their tens of thousands, leaving us without even enough honey to spread on soda biscuits we could no longer afford.

The winter following the foul brood disaster was a tough one. Angus sought work and Don Fraser, brother of the ubiquitous Billy, tried to employ him as an insurance salesman.

"It wasn't any good," Angus remembered. "I was too shy, you see. When I saw a likely prospect coming, I'd cross to the other side of the street. But once old Tommy Potts tracked me down. He was eighty-seven, blind in one eye and couldn't see out of the other, and had halitosis that could knock a horse off its feet at fifty yards. He said he was dying and needed life insurance. I sold him fifty thousand or so dollars' worth on credit but Don wouldn't honor the sale."

To make things worse, the chimney in our house's cavernous kitchen caught fire and collapsed. We escaped unscathed but had to seek refuge in another decayed structure, which Angus christened the Swamp House because it stank pervasively of rotten wood.

My mother, most long-suffering of women, was able to endure this except when visitors were expected. Then she would burn quantities of brown paper in the kitchen stove with the chimney damper tightly shut, thereby filling the house with acrid smoke. She admitted that this was exchanging one stink for another but hoped her half-asphyxiated visitors would at least be unaware of the underlying stench of mold which, to her mind, was synonymous with the "stench of poverty."

At this juncture some of our family's well-wishers came to the rescue. The librarian of the Trenton Public Library, a crotchety spinster who had run her little fiefdom with an autocratic hand for thirty years, maintaining her position by threatening to resign if anyone questioned her rule, chose to make this threat once too often. The chairman of the board took her at her word and offered the job to Angus, at the munificent salary of five hundred dollars a year.

So Angus began the career which was to engross him for the rest of his working days. And we three began to eat regularly. Leaving the Swamp House to the mold and mildew, we took up residence in two upstairs rooms rented from Mrs. White, a railroad worker's widow whose daughter had been one of my father's girls in high-school days. This choice did not please my mother. Years later she was to tell me, "He was as charming to that little sniff of a daughter as if she was a princess; and the way she looked at him was enough to make one ill." Even then I think my mother had begun to suspect she had married a rover.

My father's interest in women was surpassed only by his passion for boats, a passion he was determined his son must share. When I was a year old, he began taking Helen and me on weekend excursions aboard one or other of the several local boats owned and sailed by friends.

In July of 1923, we embarked on our first family cruise—in an ancient sailing canoe borrowed from a retired banker. It must have been built by one of Noah's sons, and hadn't been near the water since. Its sail was so thin and sere you could see through it. Nevertheless Angus dumped a little tent, some duffel and food aboard, and we set sail.

Despite the canoe's fragility, Angus drove it hard for two days toward the eastern reaches of the bay. We sailed by day and camped on the low, mosquito-haunted shores at night. By the third day, we were half-way along the coast of Big Island when a nasty black squall with thunder and driving rain hit us over the stern, and Angus made for land.

None too soon either, according to Helen. "You were like a little wet rat," she told me many years later, "too cold even to cry. I was crying, with fury. Angus knew that I never liked sailing except for short runs on sunny days with *very* little wind. But you know what your father was like when he was determined to do something dramatic."

I did not know at the time, of course, but I learned that when it came to engaging in sheer, pig-headed histrionics, Angus had few rivals. This was a characteristic which caused my mother much distress, although it did not bother me during my childhood years.

The following day it continued to rain heavily, with great gusts of wind which finally dissolved the old sail into flapping fragments. There being nothing else for it, Angus reluctantly (and with difficulty) managed to paddle us into Picton harbor. Here the voyage ended in a mutiny. My mother simply refused to go any farther in "that leaky old thing, and Bunje just a two-year-old."

Angus was then left with no alternative but to take a train to Trenton to pick up Henry, and come and get us and the canoe. The loss of face he suffered or thought he suffered in having to end the voyage so ignominiously was something for which I think he never quite forgave my mother.

Our next home was a two-bedroom apartment above a clothing store on the main street. This was not a select residential neighborhood but the rents were low and it was adjacent to the harbor, which was convenient since Angus had decided to buy a boat of his own.

He bought a seventeen-foot Akroyd sailing dinghy—a beautiful, varnished center-boarder that sailed like a witch, and cost him a quarter of his first year's salary. He christened her *Little Brown Jug** and she became the apple of his eye.

Our first cruise in *LBJ*, as she was familiarly known, took place in the summer of 1924. It should have been a pleasant saunter through the sheltered waters of the Bay of Quinte to Kingston and have taken no more than four or five days. It took ten. Angus's log chronicled the voyage with the laconic insouciance of a master mariner taking his square rigger around Cape Horn. Helen, however, recalled it with the kind of shuddering horror which might have afflicted a French gentlewoman being conveyed to the guillotine in a tumbril. I recall it as through a glass dimly, wetly.

It was an exceptionally cold summer. Thunderstorms occurred almost daily, accompanied by vicious squalls that churned the shallow waters of the bay into yellow foam. On one occasion the wind blew with gale force for thirty-six hours. High winds and high waters produced floating debris ranging from tree trunks

---

* Inspired by a popular drinking song, "Little Brown Jug, oh I love thee."

to a dead pig. One day a piece of flotsam was driven into the center-board housing, jamming the board in the "up" position. This was no problem as long as we were running free, but when a howling head wind suddenly burst upon us, *Little Brown Jug* could get no hold on the water and was blown into a vast cat-tail swamp behind Foresters Island. Here for an entire night Helen endured a local version of the travails of Katharine Hepburn aboard *The African Queen*. Meanwhile, Helen's Humphrey Bogart flailed about in the swamp muck under the hull trying to free the center-board. Had this in fact been Africa, Angus would have been a goner. The crocodiles would have got him. And if they had, I suspect my mother might not have mourned overmuch.

LBJ was a racing machine built for day sailing. She had no cabin and offered no more shelter to man, woman, child, food, or bedding than could be found in a cubby-hole under her tiny foredeck. There was barely sufficient space for me in this cramped little cave. And it seemed never to stop raining or, if it did, the wind blew so hard that spray soaked everything anyway.

I recall sitting on the floorboards with bilge water sloshing over my bare legs and around my naked bum. More water dribbled down through a seam in the foredeck a few inches above my head, and still more came pelting in through the entrance to my cave whenever a rain squall drove against the sail. Being themselves soaking wet most of the time, there was little enough my parents could do for me.

Helen put a thick woolen sweater on my top but there was no use clothing the rest of me, which was sitting in the soup. There were some crayfish crawling around and I amused myself playing with them.

"When I peeped in at you," Helen remembered, "I thought of *Water Babies* and wondered if you might sprout gills."

I appreciated those crayfish, and also some pollywogs, but I doubt that I was particularly happy slithering helplessly about on the floorboards whenever *Little Brown Jug* came about, or being jounced mercilessly up and down as she butted her way into what must have been quite formidable waves.

The experiences I endured during this primal cruise were indelibly etched into my subconscious. Alas, my poor father! In attempting (in his spartan way) to inculcate a love of the sea in his son, he but succeeded in instilling in me a deeply rooted distrust of the sailing life, as anyone who has read *The Boat Who Wouldn't Float* will know.

The immediate result of that ordeal was a protracted trial of wills between my parents. Although occasionally and reluctantly inveigled into going day sailing, Helen resolutely refused to go cruising again unless in a much larger boat, one with a comfortable and waterproof cabin, and an engine that could hurry the vessel into safe harbor in times of storm and peril.

She was not being selfish. Selfishness was no part of her nature; she was worried about the perceived threat to *my* survival. Although prepared to be almost infinitely malleable on her own account, she could become an intractable obstacle if she felt my well-being was in jeopardy. "Balky as a bloody mule!" was how my disgruntled father put it.

Being used to getting his own way, Angus held out for an entire year. Then, near summer's end of 1925, he capitulated. He sold *LBJ* and bought an antiquated twenty-six-foot, Lake Ontario fish boat. She was propelled by a 10-horsepower, single-cylinder gasoline engine and did not even have a sail. She was, in fact, that ultimate anathema of all true sailor men—a "*stink-pot!*" *Angus Mowat had bought a power boat!* Neptune surely shuddered. This was not mere capitulation; it was abject surrender. Or so it seemed.

"Your father was such a cunning man," Helen remembered sadly. "The artful dodger!" He did build a cabin on *Stout Fella* (so-called because she was) and it was quite comfortable. But he either couldn't or *wouldn't* make the engine run properly. It was always stopping at the most awkward moments, leaving us drifting about for hours until some kind soul gave us a tow. Angus didn't say much about these contretemps, except to swear at the engine, but sometimes he would mutter loudly enough for us to hear, "If only this was a sailboat, we could get home on our own."

One summer day in my fifth year, *Stout Fella* was belching her noisy way eastward down the bay toward the combined causeway and bridge which connects the almost-island of Prince Edward County to the town of Belleville on the mainland.

The movable central span was already swinging to allow a west-bound tug towing a string of coal barges to pass through. Angus concluded (or so he told us) that there would be ample time for us to slip through ahead of the tug, so he headed *Stout Fella* for the gap. Just as we entered it, the engine gave a terrible backfire and quit.

When the engine failed, I was standing near the bow feeling superior to the passengers in a long line of motor vehicles and horse-drawn wagons backed up on both sides of the swinging span. *Stout Fella* lost way and did a slow pirouette until she lodged sideways across the gap—her bow aground on some buffer logs edging one bridge pier and her stern jammed against the casing of the opposite pier.

The tug (the *M. Sicken* out of Trenton) sheered off from the gap, her hoarse whistle giving full vent to her skipper's outrage. Car drivers began to blow their horns. The bridge master, a retired lake captain with a flowing white beard, shot out of his little cubicle and hung over the railing ten feet above our heads.

"Gol durn you, Mowat, you done that a-purpose!" he bellowed. "Now you git that old strawberry crate out of there or by the livin' Jesus I'll have the Belleville garbage truck come and git ye!"

His irritation was warranted. This was a hot Saturday morning and the causeway was full of produce-laden farmers' trucks bound for the Belleville market. The raucous blare and tootle of their horns filled the air. Horses neighed their distress. Red-faced men and women stomped from their vehicles toward the gap, angrily waving their arms at us.

In the face of all this hostility, I retreated uncertainly to the cockpit. Humiliated beyond endurance, Helen burst into tears and fled into the little cabin, slamming the companionway hatch behind her. The comments from above became even more derisive.

"Why'n't you just pull the plug and let that bathtub sink?" someone shouted.

"Ain't no bathtub! Looks more like granddad's privy what went adrift in the Big Storm last fall," jeered another.

One particularly irate farmer, who had been to school with Angus, shouted, "Thought you was supposed to be a sailor, Mowat! What in hell are you doin' driving a god-damn *tractor?*"

The completely uncharacteristic way Angus endured this barrage leads me to believe the bridge master was correct. Nary a sharp rejoinder crossed my father's lips as, calmly and unhurriedly, he took the boat-hook and worked the vessel free. Then, almost gaily, he leapt ashore on the rocky rip-rap with a line in his hand and hauled *Stout Fella* out of the gap, clearing the way for the *M. Sicken*, whose safety valve seemed about to pop. Only then did my father respond to his tormentors.

"That's right, Johnny. I *should* have stuck to sail. Won't make *that* mistake again." And he smiled sunnily up at the crowd as its constituent parts began to head back to their vehicles.

He was still smiling as he turned to me and said, "All right, Bunje-boy. You can tell your mother it's safe to come on deck again."

That winter Angus rigged *Stout Fella* as a ketch and thereafter we sailed her almost every spring, summer, and autumn weekend, and for as much intervening holiday time as Angus could squeeze out of the library board. Since the board included three other dedicated sailors, it was generous in this regard. It was less so with money, of which in truth it had only a pittance to dispense. But we happily made do on an income which by current standards would be well below the poverty line.

We led a good life, no small part of which was lived afloat at little cost. Although we did use the "bullgine" occasionally to get us out of difficulties (it never again failed us, be it noted), for the most part the wind provided free fuel. Food was to be had for the taking (fish from the bay), or the asking (vegetables, milk, cream, butter, and eggs from the many farms along the shores). Farm wives would often give my mother fresh-made bread and pies, jars of preserves and pickles, bottles of maple syrup, a chicken or a ham, or a cut of fresh meat if an animal had been slaughtered recently.

These people would have indignantly refused money in recompense but Angus was able to reciprocate in his own way. Although most of the county farmers were passionately fond of reading, books were always in short supply, so Angus began surreptitiously lending them volumes from the Trenton Library. *Stout Fella* became a kind of forerunner to the Traveling Library trucks which now serve rural regions.

There were scores of sheltered coves and anchorages around the bay and *Stout*

Fella came to know them all. I came to know their people: dairy men, apple growers, commercial fishermen, family farmers, poachers, pot hunters, village merchants, even one or two moonshiners. For the most part they were United Empire Loyalist stock—people of Dutch and English ancestry who had fled north from the Thirteen Colonies as refugees from the American Revolution. They were people of conviction, of enduring loyalties, and of great generosity.

One of our favorite haunts was Prinyer's Cove, a tree-shaded slit in the Prince Edward County shore where we would lie lazily at anchor through days of summer content. Usually we had this hidden place to ourselves. The glittering, snarling hordes of mass-produced floating automobiles which now roil the placid waters of the bay were, as yet, unknown.

It was my job to row ashore early each morning through a dawn mist and pad barefoot up the dusty track to a nearby farm to collect a can of milk still warm from the cow. Generally I would also scoff a preliminary breakfast with the farmer's wife and her three daughters. Back aboard *Stout Fella*, I would have my second breakfast: oatmeal porridge slathered in creamy milk and drenched with maple syrup or mounded with brown sugar. Everyone knew sailors had to have hearty meals, and diabetes was not something we worried about.

At some of our "ports of call," we would moor alongside a wharf or jetty, as at Rednersville, a village consisting of three houses, one general store, and a rambling canning factory thrusting a skinny iron chimney high into the air. At harvest time, which began when the first field peas were ripe, this chimney would spout a great plume of sulphurous coal smoke, the signal for scores of wagons and old trucks laden with canning crops to converge on the plant.

Many farm kids would come along for the ride and they made festival about the dock, from which one could dive to a cool, dark depth of ten feet or more. They were frankly envious of me and "my" boat, and once a boy of about my own age offered an ancient penny (which he claimed was pirate gold) if I would let him stow away aboard *Stout Fella*.

Moving West

One gray January afternoon in 1933 Angus brought home momentous news. He had been offered the job of chief librarian in Saskatoon, Saskatchewan, a place so distant from the Ontario experience that most people, if they had heard of it at all, thought it was some sort of geographic joke. Despite the fact that there would be no increase in salary, and the Depression was deepening daily, Angus was tremendously excited. Helen did not share his enthusiasm.

"Surely you wouldn't do such a thing," she cried. "It would be like taking us to Siberia or some dreadful place like that!"

In common with most easterners, she envisaged Saskatchewan as an alien and hostile world, a frigid, windswept wilderness in winter and a featureless and dreary expanse of dusty wheat fields in summer. She believed it was inhabited (barely) by peasants from central Europe who lived in sod huts, wore sheepskin clothes, ate black bread, and practiced obscure religious rites.

She knew for a fact that the prairies were in the grip of a devastating drought, one of whose manifestations was cyclonic dust storms which whirled the topsoil off eroding farms and left their owners destitute. She had also gathered from the newspapers that the Depression was laying an even heavier hand on the prairies than on Ontario. All in all it was beyond her comprehension why anyone would want to go to Saskatchewan.

However, Angus was determined to make the move, and I backed him up. Our motives were essentially the same. We were men, and Adventure was calling.

My own image of Saskatchewan was of an enormous green plain rolling to an unimaginably distant horizon, inundated by black hordes of buffalo and inhabited by Indian tribes who rode their horses as if they were one with their steeds. My twelve-year-old's imagination assured me that the world of the Wild West was still alive.

Although I did not take part in the discussions which ensued between my parents, I was well aware of them. I knew by my mother's air of gloom and bouts of tears that she was fighting a losing battle. I was glad of it because, as each day passed, I wanted ever more desperately to go west. I closed my mind to her travail. It was not until many years later that she told me how she had felt at the time.

"You see, Farley, what Angus was asking me to do was give up not just the world I knew but most of the people who were part of my life. I would be cut off from all those I treasured most, after you and Angus. Perhaps it was very selfish of me but I wanted to stay where I felt I belonged. Going adventuring into the unknown does not attract most women, you know. It frightens most of us, or so it did me."

At the end of January, Angus tendered his resignation to the Windsor* library board, to take effect on June 30. We were committed to one of the great adventures of my life.

One of Helen's most potent arguments in her struggle to dissuade Angus from going to Saskatoon was that he would be leaving behind the world of waters and boats which had always been so much a part of him. No more cruising on the bay. No more voyaging on Lake Ontario. Saskatchewan was a "dust bowl," a semi-desert, and Angus must surely despair of such a place.

The argument was sound but it did not take into account my father's capacity for self-delusion, with which he now set about manufacturing the illusion of a maritime world in the distant west.

To begin with, he determined that we would not make the journey by train, as sensible migrants of that era did. No, we would become as one with the early pioneers and head out in a covered wagon. Although (in order to enlist my mother's romantic instincts) he initially described the proposed vehicle as a "kind of gypsy caravan," what he actually had in mind was a *prairie schooner*; one which he would design, build, and pilot himself. As captain of his own ship, with Helen and me as crew, he proposed to make the passage to Saskatoon in nautical fashion.

Through the good graces of another of his high-flying friends, Angus got

---

* The Mowats had moved to Windsor in 1930.

free use of a heated building at the Corby Distillery in Walkerville. Here, in early February, he began constructing his vessel.

There were those amongst my parents' acquaintances who thought and freely said that the choice of this locale for such an endeavor was inspired. "If Angus wasn't drunk when he got that crazy idea, he will be before he gets very far along with it," was the opinion of Alex Bradshaw, our neighbor in the next apartment. But Alex was wrong. Although my father drank whenever conditions were right he was no alcoholic. He was a man so dedicated to his dreams that not even the proximity of tens of thousands of gallons of whisky could seduce him from his purpose.

During the next six months he spent most of his weekends and holidays building a ship's cabin about eight feet wide and fifteen long, mounted on the four-wheeled frame of a Model T Ford truck. Uncompromisingly square both fore and aft, it had a cambered deck high enough to provide headroom for a tall man. Angus framed his vessel with steamed, white oak ribs and sheathed her with tongue-and-groove cedar planking, over which he stretched an outer skin of marine canvas. "Ought to be able to stand up to a hurricane," opined one of those who came to see her growing. "Yep, but it'll take a locomotive to shift her," another concluded. Angus kept his peace. He *knew*, with the assurance of perfect faith, that Eardlie* would be up to the task of hauling our prairie schooner halfway across the continent.

I shared his faith and helped him at work as far as I could—which wasn't very far. Although I loved fiddling with tools and wood, I could not then and still can't measure things with anything like the accuracy required of a craftsman. One day when I had made a cut half an inch short in a piece of wood for the caravan's frame, he said to me, quite unkindly, "Bunje, my lad, you are without doubt the roughest carpenter one man ever told another about. Why don't you take up knitting or finger-painting?"

---

* In the financially euphoric spring of 1929, Angus had felt flush enough to do away with old, black Henry and buy a car more nearly befitting his rising status. He chose a pea-green Model A Ford roadster equipped with a folding canvas top and rumble seat. He named this jaunty vehicle Eardlie, in gratitude to the dealer, Eardlie Wilmott, who had given Angus a bargain on it out of admiration for my mother.

Angus was an excellent carpenter, and he fitted out the vessel's interior with skill and cunning. The trim little galley boasted a small ice-box, a gasoline camp stove, and a tiny sink. There were two main berths in the afterquarters. A smaller, folding, pipe berth, slung across the stern, was my rookery. Built-in bookshelves, lockers, a table, and a settee completed the furnishings. The whole was made bright and airy during daylight hours by six large ports, and at night by two brass oil lamps set in gimbals. The windows—sorry, ports— were fitted with red and white striped awnings which could be demurely lowered when the vessel was at anchor.

Angus painted his new vessel green and christened her *Rolling Home*; but she was better known as Angus's Ark which, being difficult to say, was shortened to the Ark.

On Saturday morning, August 5, 1933, the Ark set sail on her maiden voyage—a trial run, as it were—to Oakville, from whence we would take our eventual departure for Saskatchewan.

The omens were not propitious. When only a few miles on our way, the unwieldy vessel (which, because she had four wheels, tended to sheer wildly from side to side) escaped my father's control and ricocheted off a curb, knocking several of the wooden spokes out of a front wheel. Angus had to drive Eardlie back to Walkerville and search out a new wheel, leaving Helen and me to explain to a crowd of the curious what the Ark was and what she was supposed to be doing. The reaction was one of incredulity.

"She'll never make it!" said an onlooker. "Nope. You'd best haul her onto the nearest bit of ground, Missus, and plant some flowers out in front, and settle down right here."

Helen might have been content to do just that but Angus returned with a new wheel, repairs were effected, and we continued to our first destination, Port Stanley on Lake Erie. We moored for the night alongside a friend's cottage and I went happily off to swim in the lake, while Helen cautiously cooked our first meal *en passage*. This consisted of scrambled eggs on toast, coffee (milk for me), more toast, and honey. As time wore on, she became somewhat more adept at coping with the galley stove which, if not carefully watched, tended to flare up and incinerate the cook.

The captain wrote in his log next morning: "A pretty sleepless night. In the next cottage, a party from Detroit made merry until 5:00 a.m. and Farleigh was seasick during the night and vomited over the side of his bunk into mine."*

I was *not* seasick. It was simply that the excitement of our departure had got to my stomach which was notoriously "delicate"—a condition which my grandmother Thomson blamed on "all those soda biscuits and honey the poor lamb had to eat when he was small."

The following day we reached Oakville, where we remained for two weeks with Angus's parents. They were then in their seventies and gloomily viewed our departure for the Far West as a final separation.

We "hauled anchor" on the morning of August 21. Angus had used some of the intervening time to adjust the tow bar so that the Ark no longer sheered about like an unbroken stallion on a slack tether. Nevertheless, she did not tamely follow Eardlie, and the Captain still had problems with the helm. "Going through London we found the narrow streets and fool street-cars a distinct nuisance," he noted angrily. I hesitate to think what the streetcar drivers must have felt about us. Certainly we must have been a trial to motorists on the open highways for they had to dawdle along behind, sometimes for miles, before finding a stretch where they might safely pass our lurching behemoth.

Because the rumble seat was packed full of luggage, I began the voyage crowded between my parents on Eardlie's narrow front seat. All of us soon grew dissatisfied with this arrangement and, after a few days of querulous discomfort, Angus asked me if I would like to ride inside the Ark itself.

What a question! Would I have liked to skipper the *Queen Mary*? Would I have liked to pilot the *Graf Zeppelin*?

---

* During our final year in Windsor, I had become increasingly unhappy with a Christian name which the other kids inevitably altered to Fart-ley. When I complained about this to my father, he proposed to solve the problem by changing the spelling. This, he claimed, would take the curse off it. So I officially became Farleigh and, as far as he was concerned, the matter was settled. Of course this attempt to disguise the obvious had absolutely no effect.

The upshot was that I traveled most of the way to Saskatoon in command of a vehicle which adopted as many guises as my imagination willed. One of these was a World War I Vimy bomber. Crouched on my pipe berth in the stem, I kept my Lewis gun (actually a Daisy air rifle) swinging from side to side as I waited for pursuing Spads or Fokkers to fly into my sights. I would insult pursuing enemy pilots with such gestures of disdain as wagging my fingers in my ears, sticking out my tongue and, yes, even thumbing my nose, before pouring a burst of machine-gun fire into their vitals.

My parents were baffled by the hostility displayed by some overtaking motorists who shook their fists at Eardlie, yelled insults, and on one memorable occasion flung a hot-dog with such accuracy that it splattered mustard all over *Rolling Home*'s bluff bows.

Angus would bare his teeth at such displays of incivility and fling pungent epithets back while Helen, who hated displays of raw emotion, cringed in the seat beside him.

In 1933 one could not drive east and west across Canada because no road yet spanned the great hump of granite and spruce forests north of Lake Superior. Consequently, we had to cross into Michigan in order to make our way westward. This we did by taking a ferry across the St. Clair River from Sarnia to Port Huron.

Since Eardlie's best speed never exceeded twenty-five miles an hour our progress was leisurely. On a good day we might run a hundred and twenty miles. We made fairly good time on pavement but gravel roads, which became the norm the farther west we went, were our bane. Poor Eardlie could not seem to get a good grip on gravel, and slithered and slid about with abandon. Nevertheless he was always game and the log is filled with entries attesting to his fortitude. "This day Eardlie hauled *Rolling Home* over a steady succession of fairly high hills on the way to Grand Rapids, and did it without even a wheeze or a cough, though he did drink an extra quart of oil." It is notable that Angus always referred to Eardlie as male, and in terms which more nearly applied to a horse than an automobile. But *Rolling Home* was *female*, as a ship must be. It seems not to have occurred to him that the idea of a horse hauling a ship across the continent was somewhat bizarre.

The route we were following required us to take a ferry across Lake Michigan, but when we arrived at the docks on the eastern side of the lake it was to find that *Rolling Home* was too high to clear the vessel's doors. We were told our only hope was to try loading her on a railroad ferry which sailed from Ludington, another port well to the north. It seemed a slim chance but the alternative—to drive all the way south around Lake Michigan through Chicago and its environs (inhabited mainly by Al Capone's ruffians, so we believed)—was not attractive. We headed north.

The men servicing the huge railroad ferry, *Père Marquette*, were amused but helpful. "We *might* put that thing [the Ark] on a flat car and ship 'er over as cargo but then she'd be too high to go through *our* loading doors. Nope, that won't do. But we've got a train to load aboard and if there's room behind the caboose we might be able to roll that thing on too."

Which is what they did. Ten men manhandled the Ark onto the rails and aboard the ferry where they lashed her tight against the caboose with Eardlie nosing up to her stern. We went on deck but Helen was concerned about our Ark.

"Whatever will the poor thing think? One minute she's a caravan, then a prairie schooner, and now a freight car. I do hope she doesn't get confused."

The crossing to the Wisconsin side of the lake took six hours and was one long delight. I was especially thrilled when the second engineer took Angus and me below and showed us the engine room. I was barefoot, having lost one shoe the day before, and Angus was in flannels.* We were sights to behold when we emerged on deck again but what a spectacle those huge steam engines were, all brass and gleaming motion and spurts of vapor.

We then showed some of the crew through *Rolling Home*, in return for which the first mate asked us to the pilot house where we spent a fascinating hour amongst the radios, compasses, and other instruments, and I was allowed to put my hands on the great mahogany steering wheel. Later, at dinner in the saloon, we met a couple from Regina, the capital of Saskatchewan, on their way home by train. They talked "west" with my parents and told us a good deal about the drought and the dust storms which awaited us.

Driving on from Manitowoc the next day, we reached Lake Winnebago, near which we anchored for the night, and *Rolling Home* became the recipient of considerable attention and admiration from the inhabitants of the nearby town. I wonder now. Was our visit the seminal factor which would one day unleash thundering hordes of Winnebago motor-homes to prowl all over North America? I devoutly hope we were not responsible for that.

Saturday, August 27, was notable because we had a strong tail wind with whose help Eardlie occasionally got up to thirty miles per hour and ran off a record passage of one hundred and seventy miles, consuming fourteen gallons of gasoline and three quarts of oil in the doing. Reaching the town of Hudson on the St. Croix River just before dusk, we anchored in the local tourist park. This dispirited acre of burned-out grass offered a superb view of the river valley, and some of the dirtiest toilets we had yet encountered. I went looking for

---

* Angus was always a natty dresser, even when embarked on a pioneering voyage such as ours. I was then and have remained quite the opposite.

birds while Helen went shopping at a nearby general store and Angus picked up a twenty-pound block of ice.

In the Thirties every town and most villages had a public tourist park which provided, usually free-of-charge, outhouses, running water (cold), fireplaces, and sometimes firewood. These refuges were much used by migrants moving about the country in search of work. One such family was in the park when we arrived. It consisted of an aged, extraordinarily tall, thin, dirty, stocking-less man; three boys from ten to fourteen in tattered overalls; two girls, quite comely in men's trousers; and a baby a few months old. They were traveling in a hopelessly dilapidated car, towing a broken-down trailer in which they carried a tattered tent and their camping gear. The girls seemed to do all the work while the old man slept. According to what one of the boys told me, they originally hailed from Texas, and had been on the road since March and were heading north to hoe potatoes.

Although sympathetic with their plight, Angus thought these people shiftless. Helen was a little frightened by them. I found them interesting and became chummy with the boys, who much admired my air rifle, but I thought them greedy for the way they devoured a plateful of cookies Helen offered them.

Much later, while reading Steinbeck's *Grapes of Wrath,* I would remember the cookie incident with a pang of shame, but at the time I had no comprehension of the miseries and degradation to which that family and several millions like them were being subjected. For them, the economic collapse of 1929 had not been a "depression" but a bottomless pit into which they had been plunged with small hope of escape. Most of the people with whom we shared the municipal "tourist" parks were, in fact, Depression refugees, desperately seeking work of whatever kind wherever they could find it. Although most seemed a cut above the family we met at Hudson, they were all enduring adversity of a severity hardly credible to most of us today.

On September 1 we were approaching Fargo, North Dakota, when, with astonishing abruptness, we found ourselves on the prairie. "Hell's bells!" cried Angus as we stared across a world with no apparent horizon. "We're at sea!"

We headed due west, into the blue, and it was goodbye pavement, goodbye hills, goodbye trees and shade and sparkling brooks. We drew our first deep breath of prairie dust. Eardlie squared his shoulders and his engine took on a deeper hum. On every hand, threshing machines were at work. Straw stacks were burning, sending blue smoke plumes into a bluer sky. Horsemen trotted across vast reaches of virgin sod where cattle grazed. Gophers popped up and down on every hand and rattlesnakes slithered into the ditches. We passed lonely, treeless, unpainted houses from which ragged children poured out to gape and wave at our swaying green house on wheels. Late in the day we stopped on top of a little hill. As far as we could judge from the road map, we could see forty miles across the prairie in every direction. It was awe-inspiring, for it seemed to be a never-ending vista.

The fascination of it for me was intensified by the stupendous numbers and varieties of animals. There were no buffalo, but gophers (ground squirrels) of several species seemed to be everywhere. Ducks by the tens of thousands clustered noisily in the few ponds and lakes (sloughs,* we would learn to call them) that still held water. Huge hawks hung in the pale air or perched on telephone poles along the road, eyeing us balefully as we trundled by raising a cloud of

---

* Slough is pronounced "slew."

dust behind us. Red-winged and yellow-headed blackbirds flowered like tropical exotics in roadside ditches; western meadowlarks sang loud and clear from the fence posts, and coveys of partridges and prairie chickens shot out of the wheat stubble like miniature rockets.

We camped near Minot and, with my trusty Daisy in hand, I took my first walk on the prairie in palpitating fear/hope that I might meet a coyote. And I did. But he was dead—long dead and desiccated from sun and wind. His lips were drawn back over white teeth in the dry rictus of a snarl, and one hind leg was firmly clamped in the grip of a rusty steel trap.

The next day I saw a live coyote slip like an ocher shadow into the tumbleweed in a coulée, but the dead coyote looms larger in memory.

We were then driving north within a day's journey of Canada. The heat was fearful and the world burned brown. We passed a sign that read "swimming 21 mi," and our hopes rose. But when we got there it was to find a miserable little alkali lake and a ramshackle and seemingly abandoned dance hall set in the bleakest, most desolate situation that could be imagined. The lake was almost literally alive with thousands of mallard ducks which were not so much "swimming" as wading about in the muck. We did not disturb them.

On September 4 we crossed the border at Portal, North Dakota. Helen and even Angus were appalled by our first view of Saskatchewan. It looked like a desert in the making. Nothing green to be seen. Rough little valleys cut through low brown hills with not a drop of water in them. Here and there in the valley banks were the mole-like black holes where people had been digging for coal but we saw no people, no cattle, not even any gophers.

Seeking a tourist camp, we got lost and ended up in an abandoned village where gaunt, gray wooden buildings leaned against each other on an empty "main street." We headed for Estevan, the nearest town shown on our map but, before reaching it, encountered a few poplars still sporting some green leaves. There was a weathered farmhouse not far away so Angus went to ask permission to camp in the grove. Mr. and Mrs. Gent graciously gave it, but pressed us to park the Ark in their farmyard instead. Angus wrote of them:

"The Gents and their farm seemed to us rather a pathetic spectacle. They are English immigrants who have been 24 years here and raised a family, all of whom have had to leave the farm. The old couple—they were not really old although both looked it—were no farther ahead than when they landed in Canada. Yet, in spite of poor crops, drought and having to board coal-miners to stay alive, they remained cheerful and optimistic. Yes, there *had* been three years of arid drought, but next year it might rain. They *had* sowed 250 bushels of wheat this year, and harvested 500. But *next* year things might be better!

"They have two cows and a little milk route in Estevan, nine miles away. They sell a hog or two each year and some fowl, and so: 'We have managed to keep off Government relief, and that is something these days.'

"Because of the drought they have to cart their drinking water from Estevan. Washing water comes in a ditch from the nearest coal mine and is black as tar. They were most insistent that we stay with them next day, which was Sunday, for a chicken dinner and seemed deeply disappointed when we had to refuse. Having heard me complain that I did not like American tobacco, Mr. Gent pressed a package of Old Chum on me and would accept no payment. I don't know why the Almighty couldn't let such folks have a little rain occasionally."

Next morning Saskatchewan showed another face. We woke in a chill gray dawn so cold we had to run the Coleman stove to heat up the cabin. We washed in cold coal water and then bade adieu to the kindly Gents and rolled out across the prairies bound north and west for Saskatoon.

But not before Mrs. Gent, cautioning me to secrecy, had slipped a fifty-cent silver piece into my pocket. I did not tell my parents about this until much later in the day. They concluded that this may well have been the only "cash money" the Gents had in hand but, after a great deal of discussion, decided not to send it back for fear of mortally offending them. Angus kept the money "in trust" for me, but not many weeks after taking over his new job, he began shipping library books to the Gents, who had mentioned that they could seldom find anything to read.

From this beginning, Angus eventually developed a traveling library scheme by means of which the Saskatoon Public Library circulated thousands of volumes to remote parts of the province where people had no other access to books. It was his contribution to easing the miseries of the Depression and it

was no mean one either. Before we left Saskatoon, the library had accumulated a fat file of letters from people who wrote that the books they had
received had meant as much to them as food.

Angus and Helen remained in touch with the Gents for several years. I shall
not forget them. They were of the enduring quality that distinguishes people
of adversity. I was to find many more like them in Saskatchewan.

Saskatoon still lay some four hundred miles to the north-west. As we slowly made
our way toward it over dusty clay and gravel roads under a brilliantly clear
autumnal sky, the face of the land began to assume a friendlier guise. Although
these prairies were also drought-stricken, they had not been so desperately rav-
aged as those in the south. The saffron-colored wheat fields rolling away on every
hand were at least yielding something in the way of crops to the men, horses,
and machines that crawled across them. There were fewer abandoned farms.
Although surrounded by glaring white pans of alkali, many of the larger sloughs
still held central pools of water which were crowded with ducks. As we
approached Regina, we began to pass small groves of aspens and poplars.*

These "bluffs," as such groves are called in the west, grew increasingly
numerous, dotting the country to give it the semblance of one vast parkland.
The weather held calm, cool, and crisp, and none of the dreaded dust storms
we had heard so much about rose to bedevil us.

Late on a mid-September afternoon we came in sight of our new home
port. Straddling the broad and muddy South Saskatchewan River, Saskatoon's
church spires, grain elevators, and taller buildings loomed on the horizon like
the masts and funnels of a distant fleet immobilized on a golden ocean.

Founded three decades earlier as a Methodist temperance colony, Saskatoon
quickly outgrew its natal influences. By the time of our arrival, it had bur-
geoned into a city of thirty thousand people embracing the beliefs and customs

---

* The closely related trembling (or quaking) aspen and cottonwood poplars are the domi-
nant trees in Saskatchewan northward to the edge of the boreal forest. Cottonwood is
so-called because, in early spring, it covers the ground beneath it with tiny seeds attached to delicate parachutes of what looks like cotton wool.

of half the countries of the western world. Many of these, especially the Doukhobors, Mennonites, Galicians, and Hutterites, would prove to be mystery distilled in the eyes of a twelve-year-old from the staid Anglo-Saxon province of Ontario.

While Angus searched for a house to rent, we lived aboard *Rolling Home* in the municipal tourist park which was attached to the city's exhibition grounds and zoo. There were no other "tourists" so we had the place to ourselves except for two camels, an ancient buffalo bull, and a pair of elk who, together, made up the population of the zoo. I was delighted with these creatures whose like I had never seen before and was convinced by their presences that Saskatoon was truly the gateway to a wilderness world.

Mutt

The Coming of Mutt

An oppressive darkness shadowed the city of Saskatoon on an August day in 1933. By the clock it was hardly noon. By the sun—but the earth had obliterated the sun. Rising in the new deserts of the south-west, and lifting high on autumnal winds, the desecrated soil of the prairies drifted northward; and the sky grew dark.

In our small house on the outskirts of the city my mother switched on the electric lights and continued with the task of preparing luncheon for my father and for me. Father had not yet returned from his office, nor I from school. Mother was alone with the somber day.

The sound of the doorbell brought her unwillingly from the kitchen into the hall. She opened the front door no more than a few inches, as if expecting the menace of the sky to thrust its way past her into the house.

There was no menace in the appearance of the visitor who waited apologetically on the step. A small boy, perhaps ten years of age, stood shuffling his feet in the gray grit that had been falling soundlessly across the city for a day and a night. He held a wicker basket before him and, as the door opened, he swung the basket forward and spoke in a voice that was husky with the dust and with the expectation of rebuff.

"Missus," he asked in a pale, high tone, "would you want to buy a duck?"

Mother was a bit nonplussed by this odd echo of a catch phrase that had already withered and shied in the mouths of the comedians of the era. Nevertheless, she looked into the basket and to her astonishment beheld three emaciated ducklings, their bills gaping in the heat, and, wedged between them, a nondescript and bedraggled pup.

She was touched, and curious—although she certainly did not want to buy a duck.

"I don't think so," she said kindly. "Why are you selling them?"

The boy took courage and returned her smile.

"I gotta," he said. "The slough out to the farm is dry. We ate the big ducks,

44

but these was too small to eat. I sold some down to the Chinee Grill. You want the rest, lady? They're cheap—only a dime each."

"I'm sorry," Mother replied. "I've no place to keep a duck. But where did you get the little dog?"

The boy shrugged his shoulders. "Oh, *him*," he said without much interest. "He was kind of an accident, you might say. I guess somebody dumped him out of a car right by our gate. I brung him with me in case. But dogs is hard to sell." He brightened up a little as an idea struck him. "Say, lady, you want him? I'll sell him for a nickel—that way you'll *save* a nickel for yourself."

Mother hesitated. Then almost involuntarily her hand went to the basket. The pup was thirsty beyond thirst, and those outstretched fingers must have seemed to him as fountains straight from heaven. He clambered hastily over the ducks and grabbed.

The boy was quick to sense his advantage and to press it home.

"He likes you, lady, see? He's yours for just *four* cents!"

During my lifetime we had owned, or had been owned by, a steady succession of dogs. As a newborn baby I had been guarded by a Border collie named Sapper who was one day doused with boiling water by a vicious neighbor, and who went insane as a result. But there had always been other dogs during my first eight years, until we moved to the west and became, for the moment, dogless. The prairies could be only half real to a boy without a dog.

I began agitating for one almost as soon as we arrived and I found a willing ally in my father—though his motives were not mine.

For many years he had been exposed to the colorful tales of my Great-uncle Frank, who homesteaded in Alberta in 1900. Frank was a hunter born, and most of his stories dealt with the superlative shooting to be had on the western plains. Before we were properly settled in Saskatoon my father determined to test those tales. He bought a fine English shotgun, a shooting coat, cases of ammunition, a copy of the *Saskatchewan Game Laws*, and a handbook on shotgun shooting. There remained only one indispensable item—a hunting dog.

One evening he arrived home from the library with such a beast in tow behind him. Its name was Crown Prince Challenge Indefatigable. It stood about as high as the dining-room table and, as far as Mother and I could judge, consisted mainly of feet and tongue. Father was annoyed at our levity and haughtily informed us that the Crown Prince was an Irish setter, kennel bred and field trained, and a dog to delight the heart of any expert. We remained unimpressed. Purebred he may have been, and the possessor of innumerable cups and ribbons, but to my eyes he seemed a singularly useless sort of beast with but one redeeming feature. I greatly admired the way he drooled. I have never known a dog who could drool as the Crown Prince could. He never stopped, except to flop his way to the kitchen sink and tank-up on water. He left a wet and sticky trail wherever he went. He had little else to recommend him, for he was moronic.

Mother might have overlooked his obvious defects, had it not been for his price. She could not overlook that, for the owner was asking two hundred dollars, and we could no more afford such a sum than we could have afforded a Cadillac. Crown Prince left the next morning, but Father was not discouraged, and it was clear that he would try again.

My parents had been married long enough to achieve that delicate balance of power which alone enables a married couple to endure each other. They were both adept in the evasive tactics of marital politics—but Mother was a little more adept.

She realized that a dog was now inevitable, and when chance brought the duck boy—as we afterwards referred to him—to our door on that dusty August day, Mother showed her mettle by snatching the initiative right out of my father's hands.

By buying the duck boy's pup, she not only placed herself in a position to forestall the purchase of an expensive dog of my father's choice but she was also able to save six cents in cash. She was never one to despise a bargain.

When I came home from school the bargain was installed in a soap carton in the kitchen. He looked to be a somewhat dubious buy at any price. Small, emaciated, and caked liberally with cow manure, he peered up at me in a nearsighted sort of way. But when I knelt beside him and extended an exploratory hand he roused himself and sank his puppy teeth into my thumb with such satisfactory gusto that my doubts dissolved. I knew that he and I would get along.

My father's reaction was of a different kind.

He arrived home at six o'clock that night and he was hardly in the door before he began singing the praises of a spring-spaniel bitch he had just seen. He seemed hardly even to hear at first when Mother interrupted to remark that we already had a dog, and that two would be too many.

When he beheld the pup he was outraged; but the ambush had been well and truly laid and before he could recover himself, Mother unmasked her guns.

"Isn't he *lovely*, darling?" she asked sweetly. "And so *cheap*. Do you know, I've actually saved you a hundred and ninety-nine dollars and ninety-six cents? Enough to pay for all your ammunition and for that *expensive* new gun you bought."

My father was game, and he rallied quickly. He pointed scornfully at the pup, and in a voice sharp with exasperation he replied:

"But, damn it all—that—that 'thing' isn't a *hunting* dog!"

Mother was ready for him. "How do you *know*, dear," she asked mildly, "until you've tried him out?"

There could be no adequate reply to this. It was as impossible to predict what the pup might grow up to be, as it was to deduce what his ancestry might have been. Father turned to me for support, but I would not meet his eye, and he knew then that he had been outmaneuvered.

He accepted defeat with his usual good grace. I can clearly remember, and with awe, what he had to say to some friends who dropped in for a drink not three evenings later. The pup, relatively clean, and already beginning to fatten out a little, was presented to the guests.

"He's imported," Father explained in a modest tone of voice. "I understand he's the only one of his kind in the west. A Prince Albert retriever, you know. Marvelous breed for upland shooting."

Unwilling to confess their ignorance, the guests looked vaguely knowing. "What do you call him?" one of them asked.

I put my foot in it then. Before Father could reply, I forestalled him.

"*I* call him Mutt," I said. And I was appalled by the look my father gave me.

He turned his back on me and smiled confidentially at the guests.

"You have to be rather careful with these highly bred specimens," he explained, "it doesn't always do to let them know their kennel names. Better to give them a simple bourgeois name like Sport, or Nipper, or—" and here he gagged a trifle—"or even Mutt."

Mutt's Early Days

During his first few weeks with us Mutt astonished us all by his maturity of outlook. He never really was a puppy, at least not after he came to us. Perhaps the ordeal with the ducks had aged him prematurely; perhaps he was simply born adult in mind. In any case he resolutely eschewed the usual antics of puppyhood. He left behind him no mangled slippers, no torn upholstery, and no stains upon the rugs. He did not wage mock warfare with people's bare feet, nor did he make the night hideous when he was left to spend the dark hours alone in the kitchen. There was about him, from the first day he came to us, an aura of resolution and restraint, and dignity. He took life seriously, and he expected us to do likewise.

Nor was he malleable. His character was immutably resolved before we ever knew him and, throughout his life, it did not change.

I suspect that at some early moment of his existence he concluded there was no future in being a dog. And so, with the tenacity which marked his every act, he set himself to become something else. Subconsciously he no longer believed that he was a dog at all, yet he did not feel, as so many foolish canines appear to do, that he was human. He was tolerant of both species, but he claimed kin to neither.

If he was unique in attitude, he was also unique in his appearance. In size he was not far from a setter, but in all other respects he was very far from any known breed. His hindquarters were elevated several inches higher than his forequarters; and at the same time he was distinctly canted from left to right. The result was that, when he was approaching, he appeared to be drifting off about three points to starboard, while simultaneously giving an eerie impression of a submarine starting on a crash dive. It was impossible to tell, unless you knew him very well indeed, exactly where he was heading, or what his immediate objective might be. His eyes gave no clue, for they were so close-set that he looked to be, and may have been, somewhat cross-eyed. The total illusion had its practical advantages, for gophers and cats pursued by Mutt could seldom decide where he was aiming until they discovered, too late, that he was actually on a collision course with them.

An even more disquieting physical characteristic was the fact that his hind legs moved at a slower speed than did his front ones. This was theoretically explicable on the grounds that his hind legs were much longer than his forelegs—but an understanding of this explanation could not dispel the unsettling impression that Mutt's forward section was slowly and relentlessly pulling away from the tardy after-end.

And yet, despite all this, Mutt was not unprepossessing in general appearance. He had a handsome black and white coat of fine, almost silky hair, with exceptionally long "feathers" on his legs. His tail was long, limber, and expressive. Although his ears were rather large and limp, his head was broad and high-domed. A black mask covered all of his face except for his bulbous nose, which was pure white. He was not really handsome, yet he possessed the same sort of dignified grotesquerie which so distinguished Abraham Lincoln and the Duke of Wellington.

He also possessed a peculiar *savoir-faire* that had a disconcerting effect upon strangers. So strong was Mutt's belief that he was not simply "dog" that he was somehow able to convey this conviction to human onlookers.

One bitterly cold day in January Mother went downtown to do some post-Christmas shopping and Mutt accompanied her. She parted from him outside the Hudson's Bay Department Store, for Mutt had strong antipathies, even in those early months, and one of these was directed against the famous Company of Gentleman Adventurers. Mother was inside the store for almost an hour, while Mutt was left to shiver on the wind-swept pavement.

When Mother emerged at last, Mutt had forgotten that he had voluntarily elected to remain outside. Instead he was nursing a grievance at what seemed to him to be a calculated indifference to his comfort on my mother's part. He had decided to sulk, and when he sulked he became intractable. Nothing that Mother would say could persuade him to get up off the frigid concrete and accompany her home. Mother pleaded. Mutt ignored her and fixed his gaze upon the steamed-up windows of the Star Café across the street.

Neither of them was aware of the small audience which had formed around them. There were three Doukhobors in their quaint winter costumes, a policeman enveloped in a buffalo-skin coat, and a dentist from the nearby Medical Arts Building. Despite the cold, these strangers stood and watched with growing fascination as Mother ordered and Mutt, with slightly lifted lip and *sotto-voce* mutters, adamantly refused to heed. Both of them were becoming exasperated, and the tone of their utterances grew increasingly vehement.

It was at this point that the dentist lost touch with reality. He stepped forward and addressed Mutt in man-to-man tones.

"Oh, I say, old boy, be reasonable!" he said reproachfully.

Mutt replied with a murmur of guttural disdain, and this was too much for the policeman.

"What seems to be the matter here?" he asked.

Mother explained. "He won't go home. He just won't go!"

The policeman was a man of action. He wagged his mittened paw under Mutt's nose. "Can't you see the lady's cold?" he asked sternly.

Mutt rolled his eyes and yawned and the policeman lost his temper. "Now, see here," he cried, "you just move along or, by the gods, I'll run you in!"

It was fortunate that my father and Eardlie came by at this moment. Father had seen Mutt and Mother in arguments before, and he acted with dispatch, picking them both up almost bodily and pushing them into Eardlie's front seat. He did not linger, for he had no desire to be a witness to the reactions of the big policeman and of the dentist when they became aware of the fact that they had been arguing with a dog upon a public street.

Arguments with Mutt were almost invariably fruitless. As he grew older he became more vocal and more argumentative. When he was asked to do something which did not please him he would begin to mutter. If he was pressed, the muttering would grow in volume, rising and falling in pitch. It was not a growl nor was it in the least threatening. It was a stubborn bumbling sound, quite indescribable.

It happened that Father was writing a novel that first winter in the west, and he was extremely touchy about being disturbed while working on it.

One evening he was hunched over his portable typewriter in the living room, his face drawn and haggard with concentration, but he was getting very little actually down on paper. Mother and I, recognizing the symptoms, had discreetly retired to the kitchen, but Mutt had remained in the living room, asleep before the open fire.

Mutt was not a silent sleeper. He snored with a peculiar penetrating sound and, being a dog who dreamed actively, his snores were often punctuated by high-pitched yelps as he galloped across the dream prairie in pursuit of a rabbit.

He must have been lucky that evening. Perhaps it was an old and infirm rabbit he was chasing, or perhaps the rabbit slipped and fell. At any rate Mutt closed with it, and instantly the living room reverberated to a horrendous conflict.

Father, blasted so violently from his creative mood, was enraged. He roared at Mutt, who, awakened harshly in the very moment of victory, was inclined to be surly about the interruption.

"Get out, you insufferable beast!" Father yelled at him.

Mutt curled his lip and prepared to argue.

Father was now almost beside himself. "I said *out*—you animated threshing machine!"

Mutt's argumentative mutters immediately rose in volume. Mother and I shivered slightly and stared at each other with dreadful surmise.

Our apprehensions were justified by the sound of shattering glass, as a volume of *Everyman's Encyclopedia* banged against the dining-room wall, on the wrong side of the French doors. Mutt appeared in the kitchen at almost the

same instant. Without so much as a look at us, he thumped down the basement stairs—his whole attitude radiating outrage.

Father was immediately contrite. He followed Mutt down into the cellar, and we could hear him apologizing—but it did no good. Mutt would not deign to notice him for three long days. Physical violence in lieu of argument was, to Mutt, a cardinal sin.

He had another exasperating habit that he developed very early in life, and never forgot. When it was manifestly impossible for him to avoid some unpleasant duty by means of argument, he would feign deafness. On occasions I lost my temper and, bending down so that I could lift one of his long ears, would scream my orders at him in the voice of a Valkyrie. But Mutt would simply turn his face toward me with a bland and interrogative look that seemed to say with insufferable mildness, "I'm sorry—did you speak?"

We could not take really effective steps to cure him of this irritating habit, for it was one he shared with my paternal grandfather, who sometimes visited us. Grandfather was stone deaf to anything that involved effort on his part, yet he could hear, and respond to, the word "whisky" if it was whispered inside a locked bedroom three floors above the chair in which he habitually sat.

It will be clear by now that Mutt was not an easy dog to live with. Yet the intransigence which made it so difficult to cope with him made it even more difficult—and at times well-nigh impossible—for him to cope with the world in general. His stubbornness marked him out for a tragicomic role throughout his life. But Mutt's struggles with a perverse fate were not, unfortunately, his alone. He involved those about him, inevitably and often catastrophically, in his confused battle with life.

Wherever he went he left deep-etched memories that were alternately vivid with the screaming hues of outrage, or cloudy with the muddy colors of near dementia. He carried with him the aura of a Don Quixote and it was in that atmosphere that my family and I lived for more than a decade.

Mutt Goes Hunting

Father had been a pot hunter since his early youth, shooting ducks primarily for food, as Bay of Quinte men had been doing since European settlement began. He was not a killer by inclination and never relished taking the life of any living thing until we moved to Saskatoon. There he became infected by the pathological dysfunction which is called "sport" hunting. Those afflicted by this disease derive pleasure from slaughtering "game" animals ranging from moose to squirrels, from doves to geese, together with all kinds of "vermin" from wolves to crows.*

Many of Saskatoon's so-called sportsmen seemed still to be in the grip of the killing frenzy which, within human memory, had led to the extermination of the buffalo and the prairie wolf, together with the virtual extinction or massive decimation of dozens of other species of prairie animals.

That Angus, a man capable of deep compassion, could ever have brought himself to join in this butchery of the innocents for pleasure's sake remains a puzzle to me, despite something he told me in later years:

"It was the *hunt*, you understand. Getting up shivering in the dark for bacon and eggs and a mug of tea, and then the sounds and smells of an autumn dawn. Sheer ecstasy! Though there was this terrible paradox about it because when you pressed the trigger and death leapt forth, the mood of almost unbearable ecstasy was shattered. Smashed. Turned into bloody slush, just like the birds we killed. The hunting was right. The killing was an abomination because it wasn't done out of need."

Those words were spoken a long time afterwards.

Not only did he become an avid sport killer in Saskatoon, he made it his business to turn me into one too. This wasn't too difficult. Nothing could have been more attractive than the opportunity to be buddy-buddy with my father in a shared enterprise.

---

* Any creature which is even suspected of preying on game animals or of competing with them for food or living space is considered vermin by sport killers, and treated accordingly.

In the fall of the year Father and I began making preparations for our first hunting season in the west. The weeks before the season opened were full of intense excitement and anticipation for me, and the ordeal of school was almost unendurable. The nights grew colder and in the hours before the dawn I would waken and lie with a fast-beating heart listening to the majestic chanting of the first flocks of south-bound geese. I kept my gun—a little twenty-gauge (the first shotgun I had ever owned)—on the bed beside me. In the sounding darkness I would lift it to my shoulder and the roof and ceiling would dissolve as the gun muzzle swung on the track of the great voyagers.

Father was even more excited than I. Each evening he would get out his own gun, carefully polish the glowing walnut stock, and pack and repack the cartridges in their containers. Mother would sit and watch him with that infuriating attitude of tolerance that women can turn into a devastating weapon against their mates. Mutt, on the other hand, paid no attention to our preparations and, in fact, he grew so bored by them that he took to spending his evenings away from home. His complete lack of interest in guns and decoys and shells and hunting clothes disgusted Father, but at the same time righteously confirmed his original estimate of Mutt.

"We'll have to hunt without a dog, Farley," he said gloomily to me one evening.

Mother, for whom this remark was actually intended, rose to the bait.

"Nonsense," she replied. "You've got Mutt—all you have to do is train him."

Father snorted derisively. "Mutt, indeed! We need a bird dog, not a bird brain."

I was stung by this reflection on Mutt's intelligence. "I think he must have bird dog in him *some*where," I said. "Look at all his 'feathers'—like a real English setter."

Father fixed me with a stern glance and beckoned me to follow him out to the garage. When we were safely in that sanctuary he shut the door.

"You've been listening to your mother again," he accused me in a tone that emphasized the gravity of this breach of masculine loyalty.

"Not really *listening*," I apologized. "She only said we ought to try him out, and maybe he might be *some* good."

Father gave me a pitying look. "You've missed the point," he explained. "Surely you're old enough by now to realize that it never pays to let a woman prove she's right. It doesn't even pay to give her a chance to prove it. Mutt stays home."

My father's logic seemed confusing, but I did not argue. And so that first season we went out to the fields and sloughs without a dog. In the event, it was probably just as well. Both my father and I had a great deal to learn about hunting, and the process would have been impossibly complicated had we been attempting to train a dog at the same time.

That first season conclusively demonstrated that we really needed the services of a bird dog—if not a pointer then at least a good retriever. We lost a number of partridge that were only winged and that ran for cover. On one occasion we came close to losing Father when he waded out into a quicksand slough to retrieve what later was identified as a double-crested cormorant. The memory of the lost birds and, in particular, of the quicksand sat heavily on Father through the following year and gave new weight to Mother's arguments as a new hunting season approached. She had a sublime faith in Mutt. Or perhaps she was just being stubborn.

My father's retreat was slow, and defended by rearguard actions. "Mutt's so obviously not a hunting dog!" he would insist as he retired a few more paces to the rear.

"Nonsense!" Mother would reply. "You know perfectly well that once Mutt makes up his mind, he can do anything. *You'll* see."

I do not think that Father ever publicly hoisted the surrender flag. Nothing was said in so many words, but as the next hunting season drew near, it seemed to be tacitly understood that Mutt would have his chance. Mutt suspected that something unusual was afoot, but he was uncertain as to its nature. He watched curiously as Father and I salvaged our precious hunting trousers from the pile of old clothing that Mother had set aside to give to the Salvation Army (this was an annual ritual); and he sat by, looking perplexed, as we cleaned our guns and repainted the wooden duck decoys. As opening day drew closer he began to show something approaching interest in our preparations, and he even began to forgo his nightly routine check on the neighborhood garbage cans.

Mother was quick to point out that this behavior indicated the awakening of some inherited sporting instinct in him. "He's started to make up his mind," Mother told us. "You wait—you'll see!"

We had not long to wait. Opening day was on a Saturday and the previous afternoon a farmer who had come to know my father through the library telephoned that immense flocks of mallards were in his stubble fields. The place was a hundred miles west of the city, so we decided to leave on Friday evening and sleep out at the farm.

We left Saskatoon at dusk. Mutt entered the car willingly enough and, having usurped the outside seat, relapsed into a dyspeptic slumber. It was too dark to see gophers, and it was too cold to press his bulbous nose into the slip stream in search of new and fascinating odors, so he slept, noisily, as Eardlie jounced over the dirt roads across the star-lit prairie. Father and I felt no need of sleep.

Reaching our destination at midnight, we turned from the road and drove across the fields to a haystack that stood half a mile from the slough. The penetrating warning of an early winter had come with darkness, and we had long hours to wait until the dawn. I burrowed into the side of the stack, excavating a cave for the three of us, while Father assembled the guns by the dim yellow flare of Eardlie's lights. When all was ready for the morrow Father joined me and we rolled ourselves in our blankets, there in the fragrant security of our straw cave.

I could look out through the low opening. There was a full moon—the hunter's moon—and as I watched I could see the glitter of frost crystals

forming on Eardlie's hood. Somewhere far overhead—or perhaps it was only in my mind—I heard the quivering sibilance of wings. I reached out my hand and touched the cold, oily barrel of my gun lying in the straw beside me; and I knew a quality of happiness that has not been mine since that long-past hour.

Mutt did not share my happiness. He was never fond of sleeping out, and on this chill night there was no pleasure for him in the frosty fields or in that shining sky. He was suspicious of the dubious comforts of our cave, suspecting perhaps that it was some kind of trap, and he had refused to budge from the warm seat of the car.

An hour or so after I had dozed off I was abruptly awakened when, from somewhere near at hand, a coyote lifted his penetrating quaver into the chill air. Before the coyote's song had reached the halfway mark, Mutt shot into the cave, ricocheted over Father, and came to a quivering halt upon my stomach. I grunted under the impact, and angrily heaved him off. There followed a good deal of confused shoving and pushing in the darkness, while Father muttered scathing words about "hunting dogs" that were frightened of a coyote's wail. Mutt did not reply, but, having pulled down a large portion of the straw roof upon our heads, curled up across my chest and feigned sleep.

I was awakened again before dawn by a trickle of straw being dislodged upon me by exploring mice, and by the chatter of juncos in the stubble outside the cave. I nudged my father and sleepily we began the battle with greasy boots and moisture-laden clothing. Mutt was in the way. He steadfastly refused to rise at such an ungodly hour, and in the end had to be dragged out of the warm shelter. Whatever hunting instincts he had inherited seemed to have atrophied overnight. We were not sanguine about his potential value to us as we cooked our breakfast over the hissing blue flame of a little gasoline stove.

When at length we finished our coffee and set off across the frost-brittle stubble toward the slough, Mutt grudgingly agreed to accompany us only because he did not wish to be left behind with the coyotes.

It was still dark, but there was a faint suggestion of a gray luminosity in the east as we felt our way through the bordering poplar bluffs to the slough and to a reed duck-blind that the farmer had built for us. The silence seemed absolute and the cold had a rare intensity that knifed through my clothes and left me shivering at its touch. Wedged firmly between my knees, as we squatted behind the blind, Mutt also shivered, muttering gloomily the while about the foolishness of men and boys who would deliberately expose themselves and their dependents to such chill discomfort.

I paid little heed to his complaints, for I was watching for the dawn. Shaken by excitement as much as by the cold, I waited with straining eyes and ears while an eon passed. Then, with the abruptness of summer lightning, the dawn was on us. Through the blurred screen of leafless trees I beheld the living silver of the slough, miraculously conjured out of the dark mists. The shimmering surface was rippled by the slow, waking movements of two green-winged teal, and at the sight of them my heart thudded with a wild beat. My gloved hand tightened on Mutt's collar until he squirmed, and I glanced down at him and saw, to my surprise, that his attitude of sullen discontent had been replaced by one of acute, if somewhat puzzled, interest. Perhaps something of what I myself was feeling had been communicated to him, or perhaps Mother had been right about his inheritance. I had no time to think upon it, for the flight was coming in.

We heard it first—a low and distant vibration that was felt as much as heard, but that soon grew to a crescendo of deep-pitched sound, as if innumerable artillery shells were rushing upon us through the resisting air. I heard Father's wordless exclamation and, peering over the lip of the blind, I saw the yellow sky go dark as a living cloud obscured it. And then the massed wings enveloped us and the sound was the roar of a great ocean beating into the caves of the sea.

As I turned my face up in wonderment to that incredible vision, I heard Father whisper urgently, "They'll circle once at least. Hold your fire till they start pitching in."

Now the whole sky was throbbing with their wings. Five—ten thousand of them perhaps, they banked away and the roar receded, swelled and renewed itself, and the moment was almost at hand. I let go of Mutt's collar in order to release the safety catch on my shotgun.

Mutt went insane.

That, anyway, is the most lenient explanation I can give for what he did. From a sitting start he leaped straight up into the air high enough to go clear over the front of the blind, and when he hit the ground again he was running at a speed that he had never before attained, and never would again. And he was vocal. Screaming and yelping with hysterical abandon, he looked, and sounded, like a score of dogs.

Father and I fired at the now rapidly receding flocks, but that was no more than a gesture—a release for our raging spirits. Then we dropped the useless guns and hurled terrible words after our bird dog.

We might as well have saved our breath. I do not think he even heard us. Straight over the shining fields he flew, seemingly almost air-borne himself, while the high flight of frightened ducks cast its shadow over him. He became a steadily diminishing dot in an illimitable distance, and then he vanished and the world grew silent.

The words we might have used, one to the other, as we sat down against the duck blind, would all have been inadequate. We said nothing. We simply waited. The sun rose high and red and the light grew until it was certain that there would be no more ducks that morning, and then we went back to the car and brewed some coffee. And then we waited.

He came back two hours later. He came so circumspectly (hugging the angles of the fences) that I did not see him until he was fifty yards away from the car. He was a sad spectacle. Dejection showed in every line from the dragging tail to the abject flop of his ears. He had evidently failed to catch a duck.

For Father that first experience with Mutt was bittersweet. True enough we had lost the ducks—but as a result my father was in a fair way to regain the initiative against Mother on the home front. This first skirmish had gone his way. But he was not one to rest on victory. Consequently, during the first week of the season we shot no birds at all, while Mutt demonstrated with what seemed to be an absolute certainty that he was not, and never would be, a bird dog.

It is true that Mutt, still smarting from the failure of his first effort, tried hard to please us, yet it seemed to be impossible for him to grasp the real point of our excursions into the autumnal plains.

On the second day out he decided that we must be after gophers and he spent most of that day digging energetically into their deep burrows. He got nothing for his trouble save an attack of asthma from too much dust in his nasal passages.

The third time out he concluded that we were hunting cows.

That was a day that will live long in memory. Mutt threw himself into cow chasing with a frenzy that was almost fanatical. He became, in a matter of hours, a dedicated dog. It was a ghastly day, yet it had its compensations for Father. When we returned home that night, very tired, very dusty—and sans birds—he was able to report gloatingly to Mother that her "hunting dog" had attempted to retrieve forty-three heifers, two bulls, seventy-two steers, and an aged ox belonging to a Doukhobor family.

It must have seemed to my father that his early judgment of Mutt was now unassailable. But he should have been warned by the tranquillity with which Mother received his account of the day's events.

Mother's leap from the quaking bog to rock-firm ground was so spectacular that it left me breathless; and it left Father so stunned that he could not even find reply.

Mother smiled complacently at him.

"Poor, dear Mutt," she said. "*He* knows the dreadful price of beef these days."

I continued to accompany Angus on some of his hunting forays but my enthusiasm was waning. I had begun to take as much or more pleasure in watching the ducks and upland birds in life as in shooting at them. A poem I wrote at this time indicates that the killing was making me uncomfortable.

> *Sport*
> *A flash of flame that flickers there,*
> *A rain of lead that hisses by,*
> *A deafening crash that rends the air,*
> *A wreath of smoke floats in the sky.*
>
> *A bark from the dog as it gallops past,*
> *A laugh from the man who holds the gun,*
> *The flutter of birds that seek to fly,*
> *The words: "Good work!" when the deed is done.*
>
> *A ring of feathers scattered round*
> *A quivering pulp of flesh and bone.*
> *A pool of blood on the autumn ground.*
> *A life has passed to the great unknown.*

Although I did not show Angus this poem, I think he had begun to realize that the admiring son of the huntsman father was becoming disillusioned with the game. In an attempt to rekindle my enthusiasm, he bought me a twenty-gauge shotgun of my own. I was grateful but would have been more so had he instead chosen to buy me a decent pair of binoculars.

Near the end of November, Angus made a major effort to bring me back into the fold.

The traveling library he had organized had made him acquainted with a number of people scattered about the province. One of these was a Ukrainian immigrant named Paul Sawchuk. Paul owned three-quarters of a section on the shores of an immense slough known as Middle Lake, well to the east of Saskatoon.* One Thursday toward the end of the duck and goose season, Paul phoned my father to advise him that huge flocks of Canada geese were massing on the lake at night and feeding in his stubble fields at dawn.

Angus and I had never hunted Canada geese, which are the ultimate target and supreme trophy of the water-fowler. I am sure he concluded that if we went goose hunting together we could recapture the mutual excitement and camaraderie of our first hunting trips. So he arranged for me to take Friday off from school and we set out to try our luck.

It was a cold journey. Snow already lay upon the ground and the north wind was bitter. We arrived at Middle Lake in the early evening and found a frozen wasteland. Not a tree pierced a bleak void heavy with the threat of approaching snow. The roads had become frozen gumbo tracks that seemed to meander without hope across a lunar landscape. The search for Paul's farm proved long and frigid.

His house, when we found it, was a clay-plastered, whitewashed, log shanty perched like a wart on the face of a frozen plain. It had only three rooms, each with one tiny window, yet it held Paul, his wife, his wife's parents, Paul's seven children, and two cousins who had been recruited to help him with the pigs, which were his main stock in trade.

Paul greeted us as if we were lords of the realm and took us into the bosom of his family. Mutt, who by this time had become a bird dog of some considerable pretensions, refused to be taken. Having sniffed the piggy air about the

---

* A section is one square mile.

cabin with ill-concealed disgust, he refused even to leave the car. He sat on the seat, his nose dripping, saying "Faugh!" at intervals. It was not until utter darkness had brought with it the brittle breath of winter and the wailing of coyotes close at hand that he came scratching at the cabin door.

We slept on the floor, as did most of Paul's ménage since there appeared to be only one proper bed. The floor offered some advantages because the air at the lower levels contained more oxygen. At that there was none too much and, since the windows could not be opened, the trickle of fresh air which found its way under the door was soon lost in a swirl of other nameless gases. The wood stove remained volcanic throughout the night, and our lungs worked overtime and we sweated profusely.

At 4:00 a.m. Mrs. Sawchuk cooked our breakfast, which seemed to consist of barley gruel with unnameable bits of pig floating fatly in it. Shortly thereafter, storm lantern in hand, Paul guided us down to the soggy shores of the unseen lake and out onto a low mud spit.

He had earlier dug two foxholes for us at the tip of the spit but now there was ice-encrusted water in the holes. There was also a savage wind out of the north-east and, although it was still too dark to see, we could feel the sharp flick of snow driving into our faces. Paul departed and we three settled down in our holes to await the dawn.

I cannot recall ever having felt so cold. We had found a sack for Mutt to lie on but it did him little good. He began to shiver extravagantly and finally his teeth began to chatter. Angus and I were surprised by this. Neither of us had previously heard a dog's teeth chatter but before long all three of us were chattering in unison.

The dawn, when it came at last, was gray and somber. The sky lightened so imperceptibly that we could hardly detect the coming of the morning. We strained our eyes into swirling snow squalls. Then, abruptly, we heard the sound of wings—of great wings beating. Cold was forgotten. We crouched lower and flexed numb fingers in our shooting gloves.

My father saw them first. He nudged me sharply and I half-turned my head to behold a spectacle of incomparable grandeur. Out of the storm scud, like ghostly ships, a hundred whistling swans bore down upon us on stately wings.

They passed directly overhead not half a gunshot from us. I was transported beyond time and space by this vision of unparalleled majesty and mystery. For one fleeting instant I felt that somehow they and I were one. Then they were gone and snow eddies obscured my straining vision.

After that it would not have mattered to me if we had seen no other living thing that day, but the swans were only the forerunners of multitudes. The windy silence was soon pierced by the sonorous cries of seemingly endless flocks of geese that drifted, wraith-like, overhead. They were flying low and we could see them clearly. Snow geese, startlingly white of breast but with jet-black wing tips, beat past while flocks of piebald wavies seemed to keep station on their flanks. An immense V of Canadas came close behind.

As the rush of air through their great pinions sounded in our ears, we jumped up and, in what was more of a conditioned reflex than a conscious act, raised our guns. The honkers veered directly over us and we both fired. The sound of the shots seemed puny, lost in the immensity of wind and singing wings.

It had to have been pure mischance that one of the great geese was hit for, as we later admitted to each other, neither of us had aimed. Nevertheless one fell, appearing gigantic in the tenuous light as it spiraled sharply downward. It struck the water a hundred feet from shore and I saw with sick dismay that it had been winged. It swam off into the growing storm, its neck outstretched, calling…calling…calling after the vanished flock.

Driving back to Saskatoon that night I was filled with repugnance for what we had done. And I was experiencing an indefinable sense of loss. I felt, though I could not then have expressed it, as if I had glimpsed another, magical world—a world of Oneness—and had been denied entry into it through my own stupidity.

I never again hunted for sport, nor did my father ever try to lead me back to it. Although he continued to hunt, if in increasingly desultory fashion until we left Saskatoon for good, I believe his heart, too, was no longer in it.

Battle Tactics

After several years in Saskatoon, my family moved into a new neighborhood. River Road was on the banks of the Saskatchewan River, but on the lower and more plebeian side. The community on River Road was considerably relaxed in character and there was a good deal of tolerance for individual idiosyncrasies.

Only three doors down the street from us lived a retired schoolteacher who had spent years in Alaska and who had brought with him into retirement a team of Alaskan Huskies. These were magnificent dogs that commanded respect not only from the local canine population but from the human one as well. Three of them once caught a burglar on their master's premises, and they reduced him to butcher's meat with a dispatch that we youngsters much admired.

Across the alley from us lived a barber who maintained a sort of Transient's Rest for stray mongrels. There was an unkind rumor to the effect that he encouraged these strays only in order to practice his trade upon them. The rumor gained stature from the indisputable fact that some of his oddly assorted collection of dogs sported unusual haircuts. I came to know the barber intimately during the years that followed, and he confided his secret to me. Once, many years earlier, he had seen a French poodle shaven and shorn, and he had been convinced that he could devise even more spectacular hair styles for dogs, and perhaps make a fortune and a reputation for himself. His experiments were not without artistic merit, even though some of them resulted in visits from the Humane Society inspectors.

I had no trouble fitting myself into this new community, but the adjustment was not so simple for Mutt. The canine population of River Road was enormous. Mutt had to come to terms with these dogs, and he found the going hard. His long, silken hair and his fine "feathers" tended to give him a soft and sentimental look that was misleading and that seemed to goad the roughneck local dogs into active hostility. They usually went about in packs, and

66

the largest pack was led by a well-built bull terrier who lived next door to us. Mutt, who was never a joiner, preferred to go his way alone, and this made him particularly suspect by the other dogs. They began to lay for him.

He was not by nature the fighting kind. In all his life I never knew him to engage in battle unless there was no alternative. His was an eminently civilized attitude, but one that other dogs could seldom understand. They taunted him because of it.

His pacific attitude used to embarrass my mother when the two of them happened to encounter a belligerent strange dog while they were out walking. Mutt would waste no time in idle braggadocio. At first glimpse of the stranger he would insinuate himself under Mother's skirt and no amount of physical force, nor scathing comment, could budge him from this sanctuary. Often the strange dog would not realize that it *was* a sanctuary and this was sometimes rather hard on Mother.

Despite his repugnance toward fighting, Mutt was no coward, nor was he unable to defend himself. He had his own ideas about how to fight, ideas which were unique but formidable. Just how efficacious they actually were was demonstrated to us all within a week of our arrival at our new address.

Knowing nothing of the neighborhood, Mutt dared to go where even bulldogs feared to tread, and one morning he foolishly pursued a cat into the ex-schoolteacher's yard. He was immediately surrounded by four ravening Huskies. They were a merciless lot, and they closed in for the kill.

Mutt saw at once that this time he would have to fight. With one quick motion he flung himself over on his back and began to pedal furiously with all four feet. It looked rather as if he were riding a bicycle built for two, but upside down. He also began to sound his siren. This was a noise he made— just how, I do not know—deep in the back of his throat. It was a kind of frenzied wail. The siren rose in pitch and volume as his legs increased their r.p.m.'s, until he began to sound like a gas turbine at full throttle.

The effect of this unorthodox behavior on the four Huskies was to bring them to an abrupt halt. Their ears went forward and their tails uncurled as a look of pained bewilderment wrinkled their brows. And then slowly, and one by one, they began to back away, their eyes uneasily averted from the distressing spectacle before them. When they were ten feet from Mutt they turned as one dog and fled without dignity for their own back yard.

The mere sight of Mutt's bicycle tactics (as we referred to them) was usually sufficient to avert bloodshed, but on occasion a foolhardy dog would refuse to be intimidated. The results in these cases could be rather frightful, for Mutt's queer posture of defense was not all empty bombast.

Once when we were out hunting gophers Mutt was attacked by a farm collie who, I think, was slightly mad. He looked mad, for he had one white eye and one blue one, and the combination gave him a maniac expression. And he acted mad, for he flung himself on the inverted Mutt without the slightest hesitation.

Mutt grunted when the collie came down on top of him, and for an instant the tempo of his legs was slowed. Then he exerted himself and, as it were, put on a sprint. The collie became air-borne, bouncing up and down as a rubber ball bounces on the end of a water jet. Each time he came down he was raked for and aft by four sets of rapidly moving claws, and when he finally fell clear he was bleeding from a dozen ugly scratches, and he had had a bellyful. He fled. Mutt did not pursue him; he was magnanimous in victory.

Had he been willing to engage deliberately in a few such duels with the neighborhood dogs, Mutt would undoubtedly have won their quick acceptance. But such was his belief in the principles of nonviolence—as these applied to other dogs, at least—that he continued to avoid combat.

The local packs, and particularly the one led by the bull terrier next door, spared no pains to bring him to battle, and for some time he was forced to stay very close to home unless he was accompanied by Mother or by myself. It was nearly a month before he found a solution to this problem.

The solution he eventually adopted was typical of him.

Almost all the back yards in Saskatoon were fenced with vertical planking nailed to horizontal two-by-fours. The upper two-by-four in each case was usually five or six feet above the ground, and about five inches below the projecting tops of the upright planks. For generations these elevated gangways had provided a safe thoroughfare for cats. One fine day Mutt decided that they could serve him too.

I was brushing my teeth after breakfast when I heard Mutt give a yelp of pain and I went at once to the window and looked out. I was in time to see him laboriously clamber up on our back fence from a garbage pail that stood by the yard gate. As I watched he wobbled a few steps along the upper two-by-four, lost his balance, and fell off. Undaunted he returned at once to the garbage pail and tried again.

I went outside and tried to reason with him, but he ignored me. When I left he was still at it, climbing up, staggering along for a few feet, then falling off again.

I mentioned this new interest of his during dinner that night, but none of us gave it much thought. We were used to Mutt's peculiarities, and we had no suspicion that there was method behind this apparent foolishness. Yet method there was, as I discovered a few evenings later.

A squad of Bengal lancers, consisting of two of my friends and myself armed with spears made from bamboo fishing rods, had spent the afternoon riding up and down the back alleys on our bicycles hunting tigers (alley cats). As suppertime approached we were slowly pedaling our way homeward along the alley behind River Road when one of my chums, who was a little in the lead, gave a startled yelp and swerved his bike so that I crashed into him, and we fell together on the sun-baked dirt. I picked myself up and saw my friend pointing at the fence ahead of us. His eyes were big with disbelief.

The cause of the accident, and of my chum's incredulity, was nonchalantly picking his way along the top of the fence not fifty yards away. Behind that fence lay the home of the Huskies, and although we could not see them, we—and most of Saskatoon—could hear them. Their frenzied howls were punctuated by dull thudding sounds as they leaped at their tormentor and fell back helplessly to earth again.

Mutt never hesitated. He ambled along his aerial route with the leisurely insouciance of an old gentleman out for an evening stroll. The Huskies must have been wild with frustration, and I was grateful that the fence lay between them and us.

We three boys had not recovered from our initial surprise when a new canine contingent arrived upon the scene. It included six or seven of the local dogs (headed by the bull terrier) attracted to the scene by the yammering of the Huskies. They spotted Mutt, and the terrier immediately led a mass assault. He launched himself against the fence with such foolhardy violence that only a bull terrier could have survived the impact.

We were somewhat intimidated by the frenzy of all those dogs, and we lowered our spears to the "ready" position, undecided whether to attempt Mutt's rescue or not. In the event, we were not needed.

Mutt remained unperturbed, although this may have been only an illusion, resulting from the fact that he was concentrating so hard on his balancing act that he could spare no attention for his assailants. He moved along at a slow but steady pace, and having safely navigated the Huskies' fence, he jumped up to the slightly higher fence next door and stepped along it until he came to a garage. With a graceful leap he gained the garage roof, where he lay down for a few moments, ostensibly to rest, but actually—I am certain—to enjoy his triumph.

Below him there was pandemonium. I have never seen a dog so angry as that bull terrier was. Although the garage wall facing on the alley was a good eight feet high, the terrier kept hurling himself impotently against it until he must have been one large quivering bruise.

Mutt watched the performance for two or three minutes; then he stood up and with one insolent backward glance jumped down to the dividing fence between two houses, and ambled along it to the street front beyond.

The tumult in the alley subsided and the pack began to disperse. Most of the dogs must have realized that they would have to run halfway around the block to regain Mutt's trail, and by then he might be far away. Dispiritedly they began to drift off, until finally only the bull terrier remained. He was still hurling himself at the garage wall in a paroxysm of fury when I took myself home to tell of the wonders I had seen.

From that day forth the dogs of the neighborhood gave up their attempts against Mutt and came to a tacit acceptance of him—all, that is, save the bull terrier. Perhaps his handball game against the fence had addled his brain, or it may be that he was just too stubborn to give up. At any rate he continued to lurk in ambush for Mutt, and Mutt continued to avoid him easily enough, until the early winter when the terrier—by now completely unbalanced—one day attempted to cross the street in pursuit of his enemy and without bothering to look for traffic. He was run over by an old Model T.

Mutt's remarkable skill as a fence walker could have led to the leadership of the neighborhood dogs, had that been what he desired, for his unique talent gave him a considerable edge in the popular game of catch-cat; but Mutt remained a lone walker, content to be left to his own devices.

He did not give up fence walking even when the original need had passed. He took a deep pride in his accomplishment, and he kept in practice. I used to show him off to my friends, and I was not above making small bets with strange boys about the abilities of my acrobatic dog. When I won, as I always did, I would reward Mutt with candy-coated gum. This was one of his favorite confections and he would chew away at a wad of it until the last vestige of mint flavor had vanished, whereupon he would swallow the tasteless remnant. Mother thought that this was bad for him, but as far as I know, it never had any adverse effect upon his digestive system, which could absorb most things with impunity.

Vignettes of Travel

The Mowat family was a restless one—or at least my father was a restless one. Mother would have been content to stay quietly in almost any of the places that were temporarily home to us, but Father always yearned for far horizons.

During the Saskatoon period of our lives we traveled widely, from Churchill on Hudson Bay, to Vancouver on the Pacific shores. We traveled the hard way, too, for a librarian is always underpaid. However, the lessons I learned from the vicissitudes of those journeys have stood me in good stead on my own travels, for writers too are always underpaid.

In examining my memories of those excursions I am struck by the way Mutt looms so large in all of them. There was our journey to the Pacific, for example. Looking back on it now, I can recall a string of vignettes in each of which Mutt was the center of attention—while for the rest, there is nothing but an amorphous blur.

We began that journey on the June day in 1934 when I finished my last school examination paper. I still possess a snapshot taken of us as we pulled away down River Road, and when I look at it I am appalled at the manner in which we burdened Eardlie. None of your pregnant glass-and-chrome show-cases of today could have carried that load for a single mile. Eardlie could do so only because he was the ultimate result of five thousand years of human striving to devise the perfect vehicle. For there is no doubt at all but that the Model A stands at the apex of the evolution of the wheel. And it is a matter of sorrow to me—as it should be to all men—that this magnificent climax should have been followed by the rapid and terrible degeneration of the automotive species into the effete mechanical incubi which batten off human flesh on every highway of the world today.

The load that Eardlie shouldered when he set bravely forth to carry us across far mountains to the sea almost defies belief. There was a large umbrella tent tied to the spare tire; there was *Concepcion** supported high above us on a flimsy

---

* Mowat's father's sailing canoe.

rack; there were three folding wooden cots lashed to the front mudguards; on the right-hand running board (an invaluable invention, long since sacrificed to the obesity of the modern car) were two wooden crates of books—most of them about the sea; on the other running board were two trunk-suitcases, a five-gallon gasoline can, and a spare spare-tire. In addition, there were the canoe masts, sails, and leeboards; Father's Newfoundland-pattern oilskins and sou'wester; a sextant; a schooner's binnacle compass; Mother's household implements, including pots and pans and a huge gunny sack containing shreds of cloth for use in making hooked rugs; and, not least, a canvas bag containing my gopher traps, .22 rifle, and other essential equipment.

As Eardlie arched his back under the strain and carried us out of the city past the town slough, where the ducks were already hatching their young, we would have done justice to Steinbeck's descriptions of the dispossessed.

Mutt enjoyed traveling by car, but he was an unquiet passenger. He suffered from the delusion, common to dogs and small boys, that when he was looking out the right-hand side, he was probably missing something far more interesting on the left-hand side. In addition, he could never be quite sure whether he preferred the front seat—and looking forward—or the rumble seat—and looking backward. Mutt started out up front with Mother and Father, while I had the rumble seat; but we had not gone five miles before he and Mother were at odds with one another. They both wanted the outside berth, and whichever one was temporarily denied it would growl and mutter and push, until he or she gained his or her ends.

Before we had been driving for an hour Mother lost her patience and Mutt was exiled to the rumble seat.

Riding in the rumble did strange things to him, and I have a theory that his metabolism was disturbed by the enforced intake of air under pressure from the slip stream, so that he became oxygen drunk. He would grow wild-eyed and, although not normally a drooling dog, he would begin to salivate. Frequently he would stand up with his front feet on the back of Mother's neck, and he would drool on her until, driven to extremes, she would poke him sharply on the chin, whereupon he would mutter, and come back to drool on me.

But his favorite position, when he became really full of oxygen, was to extrude himself gradually over one of the rear mudguards until there was nothing of him remaining in the car except his hind feet and his tail. Here he would balance precariously, his nose thrust far out into the slip stream and his large ears fluttering in the breeze.

The prairie roads were indescribably dusty, and his nose and eyes would soon become so clogged that he would be almost blind, and incapable of smelling a dead cow at twenty paces. He did not seem to mind, but like a misshapen and misplaced figurehead he would thrust farther outward until he passed the point of balance. Then only my firm grip on his tail could prevent disaster, and on one occasion, when my grip relaxed a little, he became airborne for a moment or so before crashing to the road behind us.

When this happened we thought we had lost him forever. By the time Father got the car stopped, Mutt was a hundred yards in the rear, spread-eagled in the center of the road, and screaming pitifully. Father assumed the worst, and concluded that the only thing to do was to put the poor beast out of his misery at once. He leaped out of the car and ran to a blacksmith's shop that stood by the roadside, and in a few minutes returned waving the blacksmith's old revolver.

He was too late. While he had been out of sight, Mutt had spotted a pair of heifers staring at him over the fence, and had hastily picked himself up to give vociferous chase.

Although he suffered no lasting injuries from this mishap, there was one minor consequence that allowed me to make a place for myself in the family annals by subsequently reporting that "Mutt was so scared he went to the bathroom in his pants."

Because of the dust we three human travelers were equipped with motorcyclists' goggles. Father decided one evening that this was favoritism, and that Mutt should have the same protection. We were then entering the outskirts of a place called Elbow, a typical prairie village with an unpaved main street as wide as the average Ontario farm, and with two rows of plank-fronted buildings facing each other distantly across this arid expanse. The drugstore was the only place still open when we arrived.

Father, Mutt, and I entered the shop together, and when an aged clerk appeared from the back premises, my father asked him for driving goggles.

The old fellow searched for a long time and finally brought us three pairs that had been designed and manufactured in the first years of the automobile era. They seemed to be serviceable and without more ado Father began trying them on Mutt.

Happening to glance up while this was going on, I met the clerk's gaze. He was transfixed. His leathered face had sagged like a wet chamois cloth and his tobacco-stained stubs seemed ready to fall from his receding lower jaw.

Father missed this preliminary display, but he was treated to an even better show a moment later when he got briskly to his feet, holding the second pair of goggles.

"These will do. How much are they?" he asked. And then suddenly remembering that he had forgotten to pack his shaving kit before leaving Saskatoon, he added, "We'll want a shaving brush, soap, and a safety razor too."

The old man had retreated behind his counter. He looked as if he was going to begin weeping. He pawed the air with one emaciated hand for several seconds before he spoke.

"Oh, Gawd!" he wailed—and it was a real prayer. "Don't you tell me that dawg *shaves*, too!"

We had to improvise a special harness for the goggles because of the unusual shape of Mutt's head, but they fitted him tolerably well, and he was pleased with them. When they were not in use we would push them up on the lift of his brow, but in a few days he had learned how to do this for himself, and he could pull them down again over his eyes in time of need. Apart from the effect they had on unimaginative passers-by, Mutt's goggles were an unqualified success. However, they did not give him protection for his nose and one day he met a bee at forty miles an hour. The left side of Mutt's already bulbous nose swelled hugely. This did not inconvenience him too severely, for he simply moved to the other side of the car. But luck was against him and he soon collided with another bee, or perhaps it was a wasp this time. The total effect of the two stings was bizarre. With his goggles down, Mutt now looked like a cross between a hammerhead shark and a deep-sea diver.

When we descended into the Okanagan valley, we hoped to see a fabulous monster called the Ogo Pogo that dwells in Lake Okanagan. The monster proved reluctant, so we solaced ourselves by gorging on the magnificent fruits for which the valley is famous, and for which we had often yearned during the prairie years. To our surprise—for he could still surprise us on occasion—Mutt shared our appetites, and for three days he ate nothing at all but fruit.

He preferred peaches, muskmelon, and cherries, but cherries were his undoubted favorites. At first he had trouble with the pits, but he soon perfected a rather disgusting trick of squirting them out between his front teeth, and as a result we had to insist that he point himself away from us and the car whenever he was eating cherries.

I shall never forget the baleful quality of the look directed at Mutt by a passenger on the little ferry in which we crossed the Okanagan River. Perhaps the look was justified. Certainly Mutt was a quaint spectacle as he sat in the rumble seat, his goggles pushed far up on his forehead, eating cherries out of a six-quart basket.

After each cherry he would raise his muzzle, point it overside, and nonchalantly spit the pit into the green waters of the river.

April Passage

It was raining when I woke, a warm and gentle rain that did not beat harshly on the window glass, but melted into the unresisting air so that the smell of the morning was as heavy and sweet as the breath of ruminating cows.

By the time I came down to breakfast the rain was done and the brown clouds were passing, leaving behind them a blue mesh of sky with the last cloud tendrils swaying dimly over it. I went to the back door and stood there for a moment, listening to the roundelay of horned larks on the distant fields.

It had been a dour and ugly winter, prolonging its intemperance almost until this hour, and giving way to spring with a sullen reluctance. The days had been cold and leaden and the wet winds of March had smacked of the charnel house. Now they were past. I stood on the doorstep and felt the remembered sun, heard the gibbering of the freshet, watched little deltas of yellow mud form along the gutters, and smelled the sensual essence rising from the warming soil.

Mutt came to the door behind me. I turned and looked at him and time jumped suddenly and I saw that he was old. I put my hand on his grizzled muzzle and shook it gently.

"Spring's here, old-timer," I told him. "And who knows—perhaps the ducks have come back to the pond."

He wagged his tail once and then moved stiffly by me, his nostrils wrinkling as he tested the fleeting breeze.

The winter past had been the longest he had known. Through the short-clipped days of it he had lain dreaming by the fire. Little half-heard whimpers had stirred his drawn lips as he journeyed into time in the sole direction that remained open to him. He had dreamed the bitter days away, content to sleep.

As I sat down to breakfast I glanced out the kitchen window and I could see him moving slowly down the road toward the pond. I knew that he had gone to see about those ducks, and when the meal was done I put on my rubber boots, picked up my field glasses, and followed after.

The country road was silver with runnels of thaw water, and bronzed by the sliding ridges of the melting ruts. There was no other wanderer on that road, yet I was not alone, for his tracks went with me, each pawprint as familiar as the print of my own hand. I followed them, and I knew each thing that he had done, each move that he had made, each thought that had been his; for so it is with two who live one life together.

The tracks meandered crabwise to and fro across the road. I saw where he had come to the old TRESPASSERS FORBIDDEN sign, which had leaned against the flank of a supporting snowdrift all the winter through, but now was heeled over to a crazy angle, one jagged end tipped accusingly to the sky, where flocks of juncos bounded cleanly over and ignored its weary threat. The tracks stopped here, and I knew that he had stood for a long time, his old nose working as he untangled the identities of the many foxes, the farm dogs, and the hounds which had come this way during the winter months.

We went on then, the tracks and I, over the old corduroy and across the log bridge, to pause for a moment where a torpid garter snake had undulated slowly through the softening mud.

There Mutt had left the road and turned into the fallow fields, pausing here and there to sniff at an old cow flap, or at the collapsing burrows left by the field mice underneath the vanished snow.

So we came at last to the beech woods and passed under the red tracery of budding branches where a squirrel jabbered its defiance at the unheeding back of a horned owl, brooding somberly over her white eggs.

The pond lay near at hand. I stopped and sat on an upturned stump and let the sun beat down on me while I swept the surface of the water with my glasses. I could see no ducks, yet I knew they were there. Back in the yellow cattails old greenhead and his mate were waiting patiently for me to go so that they could resume their ponderous courtship. I smiled, knowing that they would not long be left in peace, even in their secluded place.

I waited and the first bee flew by, and little drifting whorls of mist rose from the remaining banks of snow deep in the woods. Then suddenly there was the familiar voice raised in wild yelping somewhere among the dead cattails. And then a frantic surge of wings and old greenhead lifted out of the reeds, his mate behind him. They circled heavily while, unseen beneath them, Mutt plunged among the tangled reeds and knew a fragment of the ecstasy that had been his when guns had spoken over other ponds in other years.

I rose and ambled on until I found his tracks again, beyond the reeds. The trail led to the tamarack swamp and I saw where he had stopped a moment to snuffle at the still-unopened door of a chipmunk's burrow. Nearby there was a cedar tangle and the tracks went round and round beneath the boughs where a ruffed grouse had spent the night.

We crossed the clearing, Mutt and I, and here the soft black mold was churned and tossed as if by a herd of rutting deer; yet all the tracks were his. For an instant I was baffled, and then a butterfly came through the clearing on unsteady wings, and I remembered. So many times I had watched him leap, and hop, and circle after such a one, forever led and mocked by the first spring butterflies. I thought of the dignified old gentleman of yesterday who had frowned at puppies in their play.

Now the tracks led me beyond the swamp to the edge of a broad field and here they hesitated by a groundhog's hole, unused these two years past. But there was still some faint remaining odor, enough to make Mutt's bulbous muzzle wrinkle with interest, and enough to set his blunt old claws to scratching in the matted grass.

He did not tarry long. A rabbit passed and the morning breeze carried its scent. Mutt's trail veered off abruptly, careening recklessly across the soft and yielding furrows of October's plow, slipping and sliding in the frost-slimed troughs. I followed more sedately until the tracks halted abruptly against a bramble patch. He had not stopped in time. The thorns still held a tuft or two of his proud plumes.

And then there must have been a new scent on the wind. His tracks moved off in a straight line toward the country road, and the farms which lie beyond it. There was a new mood on him, the ultimate spring mood. I knew it. I even knew the name of the little collie bitch who lived in the first farm. I wished him luck.

I returned directly to the road, and my boots were sucking in the mud when a truck came howling along toward me, and passed in a shower of muddy water.

I glanced angrily after it, for the driver had almost hit me in his blind rush. As I watched, it swerved sharply to make the bend in the road and vanished from my view. I heard the sudden shrilling of brakes, then the roar of an accelerating motor—and it was gone.

I did not know that, in its passing, it had made an end to the best years that I had lived.

In the evening of that day I drove out along the road in company with a silent farmer who had come to fetch me. We stopped beyond the bend, and found him in the roadside ditch. The tracks that I had followed ended here, nor would they ever lead my heart again.

It rained that night and by the next dawn even the tracks were gone, save by the cedar swamp where a few little puddles dried quickly in the rising sun. There was nothing else, save that from a tangle of rustling brambles some tufts of fine white hair shredded quietly away in the early breeze and drifted down to lie among the leaves.

The pact of timelessness between the two of us was ended, and I went from him into the darkening tunnel of the years.

The Others

Discovering the Others

In 1929, Mowat and his family were living in Belleville, Ontario. It was here that his interest in "the Others" was kindled. He lived next door to a family consisting of a widow and her five daughters, with whom Mowat used to play.

I had one unforgettable experience in their house. I was daydreaming in a swing sofa on their porch when a sudden movement caught my eye. I looked up to see a huge spider in the center of its web battling an equally enormous hornet. The duel was taking place only a hand's breadth away, and I felt myself being drawn directly into the world of the combatants and, in some inexplicable way, associated with them. I watched in wonderment as the velvet-clad black spider feinted warily, avoiding the dagger thrusts of the golden hornet's sting. Suddenly the spider drove its curved jaws—in the tips of which tiny jewels of liquid poison gleamed—into the back of the hornet's neck. At the same instant, the hornet curved its abdomen and buried its dagger in the spider's belly. The web, which had been shaking wildly, grew still as death overwhelmed the duelists. And I slowly emerged from something akin to a trance having, for the first time in my life, consciously entered into the world of the Others—that world which is so infinitely greater than the circumscribed world of Man.

From this time forward, non-human animals increasingly engrossed my interest, both in daily life and in my reading. I had already read my way through the anthropomorphic confections represented by the *Uncle Wiggly* series, Beatrix Potter, Mother Goose, Aesop's Fables, the Christopher Robin books, and *The Wind in the Willows*. Now I began seeking stronger meat. The Dr. Doolittle books held me for a time but I soon moved on to Kipling's *Just So Stories* and, in the realms of my imagination, became another Mowgli. I also read everything about the Others written by Ernest Thompson Seton and Charles G. D. Roberts, whose animal characters were not always shaped in the human form but were sometimes allowed to be themselves.

Saskatoon, 1935

The need to find a refuge near water returned as summer neared. This time the Mowats made no distant forays. We hauled the caravan to a site on the edge of the river six miles south of Saskatoon. The land, which had been virgin prairie not long since, was owned by the Saskatoon Country Club. Its members had built a golf course on the level ground above the river valley, leaving a broad swath of alluvial flood plain along the edge of the river undisturbed. This thickly wooded shelf had remained much as it must have been when native people were its only human visitors. Portions of the narrow track worn by these not-so-distant travelers and their horses along the river route were still discernible. An overgrown clearing close to the river and to a little clear-water spring had doubtless been used by them as a camping place since ancient times.

It was into this clearing that, with the help of a farm horse, we hauled the caravan. Having cleared away the brush, we set up an umbrella tent nearby. This became my private quarters. Then we built a stone fireplace, a trestle dining table, and a carefully concealed privy consisting of a deep trench spanned by a peeled poplar log that served as a seat. At the river's edge we constructed

a flimsy wharf—which was washed away by the fast-rising river after every significant rainfall. Near it we raised a platform of logs upon which a ten-foot, flat-bottomed dinghy Angus had built during the winter could weather the floods.

Also by the shore was a brush-roofed shelter for the use of bathers or simple loiterers. Angus called it a "go-down," and it became my mother's favorite retreat. From it one could look out across the gleaming half-mile width of the Saskatchewan. Streaked with sandbars, the river waters rolled past like an undulating satin ribbon. Ancient cottonwood and balm of Gilead trees towered over all, their shimmering leaves shading and cooling us as we lazed below them in the blistering heat of mid-summer.

This special place became our home away from home for as long as we continued to live in Saskatoon. What follows is a reconstruction from my notes of a day spent there in late June of 1935.

The darn chipmunks wake me at dawn. Four or five of them have made my tent the center of their world. It hasn't got a floor, so they pop in and out under the walls whenever they please. Mutt won't sleep in here any more because they walk all over him. One has made a nest in a little old tin trunk I found up at the club barn and hauled down here to keep stuff in. She comes right at me with her tail stuck straight up if I even touch the trunk; then all the rest hear her chatter and come in to cuss me out. Mostly they live outside but first thing every morning they gather inside to see what crumbs I've left. And there'd better be some crumbs! If not, they'll go scooting right over my face looking for grub.

Nobody else is up. I pull on my shorts and Mutt joins me from under the caravan and we go down to the river. The sun is just climbing into sight and a little mist is lying along the shore. We wade out into the water and, just for the heck of it, Mutt splashes toward a Great Blue Heron fishing on the nearest sandbank. It goes "Gwaaawk!" and flies off around the next bend where it's more private.

While I'm standing there, knee-deep, one of the bank beavers swims by. He knows me well enough by now so he doesn't even slap his tail. I try to

*join him but he can swim twice as fast as me and anyway he dives. I stick
my head under but the water is so muddy I can't see anything. How does
he see where he's going underwater?*

*When we get back to camp Dad is up and dressed and cooking break-
fast on the Coleman stove. He has to go to work in Saskatoon. Mum
doesn't, so she sleeps in. He and I eat our porridge at the log table and
McPhail,* the big, gray ground squirrel who lives under it, comes and stands
on my bare foot until I give him a piece of toast. Dad says I should make
him work for his food but what can he do? He is such a lump. Even the
Magpies take scraps away from him. They aren't here for breakfast today
so I'd better take a look at their nest and see if it's all right. The Hunters
Club in town is death on Crows and they live outside today so I'd better
take a look at their nest and see if it's all right. The Hunters Club in town
is death on Crows and Magpies, and Hawks and Owls too, and pays kids
a bounty for their eggs.*

*Dad walks up the trail and I hear Eardlie start to snort and they're off
to work. It's time to get my field glasses, my bird bands and my notebook,
and start doing my nest check. Today Mutt and me begin at the big cottonwood stub a mile up river. The eggs of the Sparrow Hawk nesting in an
old Woodpecker hole there are going to be hatching any day. She's got so
tame I can reach in and lift her right off the eggs and out the hole, and she
doesn't even scratch. Which she certainly did the first time when I put a
hand on her leg.***

*I guess wild animals get used to anything that doesn't try to hurt them.
At least, some surely do. Now, when I climb her tree in Dead Cow Bluff,
the Long-eared Owl sits tight on her nest and just turns her head and
looks me right in the eyes as if to say, "You again? What do you want this*

---

* Named by Angus in honor of a pompous member of the public library board.

** Very few bands are ever recovered because the birds carrying them do not die conven-
iently for people to find them. However, on February 5, 1936, a man named Ernest
Mica shot a sparrow hawk near Flatonia, Texas. She had a band on her leg and Mica
returned it to Washington. It was the band I had placed on the little hawk who had
nested in the old cottonwood stub.

time?" Or maybe she's looking to see if I've brought along another Star-nosed Mole like the one the caddies killed up at the club last week and I put in her nest.

I check the ten nests I know about along this part of the river bank: 4 Wrens, an Orange Crowned Warbler, a Yellow Warbler, 2 Catbirds, the Sparrow Hawk and a Red-tailed Hawk. Mostly their eggs have already hatched. The three young Red-tails are still covered with fuzz but are old enough to roll over on their backs and stick their claws up at me. In a couple more days I'll put on their bands. Today I just count the bits and pieces of about a dozen gophers in and around the edges of their nest. I throw a couple of bits down to Mutt just for a joke but he won't even give them a sniff. He likes his dinner cooked.

We finish with the river-side nests and climb up the bank near the old army rifle range. Scratch Eye Bluff is first and Mutt scurries ahead, leading the way. Last week we met a coyote here and it was just lucky for old Mutt the coyote had other business. Or maybe not. Maybe Mutt could have made friends with him but I wouldn't want to bet on it.

Although this is only a small bluff, about as big as a baseball diamond, it's got two Crows' nests and a Magpie's nest in it. All three families get along somehow. But they always gang up on me and Mutt, though they must know darn well by now we're not trouble. There's also a Loggerhead Shrike's nest in the diamond willows beside the bluff and both the Shrikes like to get into the act too. Scratch Eye can be pretty noisy when they all get going!

It takes us a while to check out all the nests in the patch of nice, fresh, green prairie and bluffs between here and the road. A pair of Kingbirds, Brown Thrashers, 2 more pairs of Crows, 4 of Flickers, one each of Brewer's Blackbirds, Meadowlarks, and a couple of pairs of Vesper Sparrows all have nests in around here. Some aren't doing too well. Something got one of the Sparrows and ate her and her eggs. Something else got into a Flicker hole and smashed all the eggs but one. But Flickers are tough. She'll just go on laying until she's got a full clutch again.

Now we cross the road onto the golf links. Nobody is out playing yet but I see one of the caddies I know, Bruce Billings. He lives on a fox farm between here and town, and we kind of like each other. He gives me a wave and I wave back as I go into Hang-Up Bluff. I call it that because a couple of weeks ago I got hung up there. I had climbed up to a Flicker's hole and put my arm in right to the elbow to count her eggs when the stub I was standing on broke off. It dropped me down with my feet swinging and my arm hooked in the hole. For a while I was scared I'd never get free but then I managed to shinny up far enough to get my arm out. It was pretty sore for a while.

Bat Bluff is next. That's where I really got surprised. I stuck my hand into what I thought was a Flicker's nest and poked my finger into a mess of needles. Or that's what it felt like. But it was a bat, and a big one too. When I hauled my hand out she was still holding onto my finger. It didn't really hurt so much but it made me jump—or I would have if I'd been on the ground. Anyway, she had two baby bats in that hole. I took all three of them back to camp and kept them in a wire mesh box in my tent. The mother bat didn't seem to mind. I opened the cage at night and off she'd go, hunting insects I guess. Every now and again I'd hear a little squeaky noise when she flew back into the tent to feed her young. Then, day before yesterday, she was gone and the babies with her. She must have carried them away one at a time. They were Red Bats which are very rare. She didn't go back to the old Flicker's nest. When I looked at it yesterday a pair of Tree Swallows had taken it over. They've already got their nest half built.

By now it's starting to get hot and Mutt lets me know he wants a drink so we head back for camp. Mum is washing her hair at the Go-down. She wants to know what we've seen and I tell her, and then get myself a glass of milk and some oatmeal cookies I share with Mutt and McPhail. McPhail may be afraid of Magpies but seems to think dogs are just movable tree stumps. Boy, has he got a lot to learn!

Well, that's the way the day goes. All in all, I look at forty-one nests of eighteen kinds of birds and make notes on what is happening to them all, and band eight young Crows.

Late in the afternoon Mutt and Mum and I go swimming then we row the dinghy out to the sandbars and lay there dozing in the sun. We're so *quiet a fox swims over from the other side, lands on our bar and would have walked right between us if he hadn't got our wind. Mutt tries to chase him back to his own side but he has other ideas. Mum and I are still laughing at the sight of the two of them swimming upstream against the current and not going anywhere much, when we hear Eardlie honking. Dad is home and it's time to light the fire and cook supper. He's brought sausages for us to grill and a store-made apple pie.*

All in all it's been a pretty good day when you come to think about it.

Wol and Weeps

One spring Mowat's biology teacher enlisted his aid in finding nests of great horned owls. Mowat became so enamored of these interesting birds that he brought a young one home. Later, he came by yet another young barn owl.

There were only a few more weeks left of school before the summer holidays began, and each day seemed a hundred years long. I could hear the river boiling over the sandbars as I sat at my desk, and I could smell the sticky-sweet smell of the young poplar leaves. Our school stood right beside the river, and every now and then a flock of ducks would go over the playground, *quack-quack-quacking* as if they were laughing at us for being stuck inside, while they were flying free across the wide prairie. What made it even worse, for me, was just sitting there wondering what my owls were doing.

After school I would jump on my bike and pedal like forty over the bridge and down our street. When I got close to home I would give a couple of owl-whoops to let Wol and Weeps know I was coming. By the time I skidded into the yard and parked my bike, they would be tramping impatiently up and down the cage. As soon as the door was open they would come waddling out as fast as they could, ready for play.

Wol liked to scramble up on the back of an old lawn chair, then he would take a wild leap and try to land on my shoulder. If he missed, he would nose-

dive into the lawn; but it never bothered him much. He would hop back to the chair, climb up, and try again until finally he made my shoulder.

Weeps was different. He never believed he could do anything by himself, and so he would just sit on the lawn and whimper until I picked him up and put him on my other shoulder. I think Weeps's spirit must have been broken in the oil drum,* because as long as I knew him he was always afraid of doing things.

---

* Mowat rescued Weeps from a group of children who were terrorizing him by holding him captive in an oil drum.

With both owls riding on my shoulders I used to go down the street to where our gang played games in an empty lot. Can-the-can was a favorite game that spring; sort of a combination of baseball and football. We used an inflated rubber beach ball that belonged to Murray, and when all the kids got chasing it, Wol would get so excited he would join in too. One time he got in the way of the ball just when someone kicked it, and it knocked the wind clean out of him. The next time the ball came near him he made a jump and got hold of it with both sets of claws. There was a hissing noise and the ball went limp. Wol was pleased as punch, but *we* weren't, because it was the only ball we had.

All the kids, except Bruce and Murray, were a bit scared of the owls, so when I had them on my shoulders I could go anywhere in Saskatoon and be safe as houses. Even the tough kids down by the flour mill kept their distance when I had the owls with me. Those owls were better bodyguards than tigers.

Wol and Weeps grew fast. Weeps would eat anything he could get and still be hungry; but Wol was fussy about his food. At first Wol would only eat cooked butcher's meat, hard-boiled eggs, and fig cookies. Later on he would eat anything that came from our table, even vegetables. (All except parsnips, which he hated.) Occasionally both owls would eat a dead gopher that some kid had shot or snared as a present for them; but they didn't really like their supper raw.

By the middle of June, when they were three months old, my new pets had reached full size. Wol was a little bigger than Weeps and stood about two feet high; but his wingspread was nearly five feet across! The claws of both were about an inch long and as sharp as needles; and their big hooked beaks looked strong enough to open a tin can. Weeps was a normal owl color, sort of a mottled brown, but Wol stayed almost pure white, with just a few black markings on his feathers. At night he looked like a ghost.

Although they were grown-up now, neither of the owls seemed to know what his wings were for. Because they saw us walking around, they seemed to think they had to walk around too. Maybe if I had been able to fly, they would have learned to fly a lot sooner; but the way things were, both owls tried to do what we kids did. They saw us climbing trees, and so they took to climbing trees.

It was pretty silly to watch Wol climbing. He used to really climb. First he'd jump up to a low branch and then he'd use his beak and his claws to half-lift himself and half-shinny to the next branch. My pigeons used to circle around sometimes and watch him. They must have thought he was crazy. People sometimes thought so too. One day Wol was climbing a poplar in our front yard when a man and a woman stopped on the sidewalk and watched him, with their mouths open.

Finally the man said to me: "What on earth's the matter with that bird? Why doesn't he *fly* to the top of the tree?"

"He can't fly, sir," I replied. "He never learned how."

The man looked at me as if I were crazy too, and walked off without another word.

The day Wol actually learned to fly was one I'll remember for a long time. He had climbed a cottonwood in the back yard and had got way out on a thin little branch, and couldn't get back. You never saw an owl look so unhappy. He kept teetering up and down on the end of the branch, and *Hoo-hoo-HOOING* at me to come and get him out of his fix.

Dad and Mother came out to see what was going on, and they started to laugh; because who ever heard of a bird that couldn't get itself down out of a tree? But when people laughed at Wol it hurt his feelings and upset him.

What with the laughter, and the fact that it was suppertime and he was hungry, Wol got careless. Finally he teetered a little too far forward and lost his balance.

"Hoo-HOOOOOO!" he shrieked as he bounced through the branches towards the ground. Then, all of a sudden, he spread his wings; and the next thing any of us knew, he was flying...well, sort of flying. Not having done it before, he didn't really know what he was doing, even then.

You could tell he was just as surprised as we were. He came swooshing out of the tree like a rocket, and he seemed to be heading straight for me; but I ducked and he pulled up and went shooting back into the air again. He was still *hoo-hooing* like mad when he stalled and slid back, downward, tail-first, and hit the ground with an awful thump.

By that time I was laughing so hard I had to lie on the grass and hold my stomach. When I looked up at last, it was to see Wol stomping into his cage. He was furious with all of us, and I couldn't persuade him to come out again until next day.

At supper that night my father said: "You know, I don't believe that owl realizes that he's an owl. I believe he thinks he's a human being. You'll have to educate him, Billy."*

It wasn't quite as bad as that. Wol eventually did learn to fly pretty well, but he never seemed to like flying, or to trust it. He still preferred to walk wherever he was going.

Weeps never learned to fly at all. I tried to teach him how by throwing him off the garage roof, but he wouldn't try. He would just shut his eyes, give a hopeless kind of moan, and fall like a rock without even opening his wings. Weeps didn't believe he could fly, and that was that.

Just before school ended, Wol learned a new trick which bothered me a lot. He discovered that if he took a good swipe at it with his claws, he could tear a hole in the chicken wire of the cage. Once he learned to do this it was impossible to keep him penned up when he didn't want to be.

This worried me because there were a lot of tough alley cats, and tough dogs too, in Saskatoon. I was afraid if one of them ever got hold of Weeps or Wol, when I wasn't around, then that would be the end.

After a look at the owls' claws and beaks, Mother said she thought it would be the end of any cat or dog that tackled Wol or Weeps; but I still worried.

One night Wol had a little argument with Mutt about a bone, and Wol got mad and wouldn't come down out of his tree to go to his cage at dusk. I called him and called him, but he just ignored me, and finally I had to go off to bed and leave him out.

I slept pretty lightly that night, with one ear cocked for trouble, because I knew the cats would be about. Sure enough, just at dawn I heard a squawk and a scuffling noise outside. I hopped out of bed, grabbed my air gun, and whipped out of the house as fast as I could.

---

* Billy was the name I adopted when we moved to Saskatoon, in order to avoid the obvious variation on "Farley" coined by some of my schoolmates in Windsor.

Wol wasn't in the tree. In fact there was no sign of him anywhere in the front yard. I raced around the corner to the back, expecting to find him dead and eaten; but, instead, I found him asleep on the back porch steps. He had his feathers ruffled out the way birds do when they are asleep, and it wasn't until I got right up to him that I saw the cat.

Wol was sitting on it, and only its head and tail stuck out beneath his feathers; but enough was showing so I could see that this cat wasn't going to bother anybody any more.

I pulled Wol off, and he grumbled a little bit. I think he'd found that cats made good foot-warmers.

It was a big ginger tomcat that lived two doors down the street and belonged to a big man who didn't like kids. This cat had been the terror of the birds, other cats, and even of the dogs in our neighborhood for years.

I got a shovel and buried it at the bottom of the garden. I suppose the cat had thought Wol was some new kind of chicken. Well, he found out differently.

Dogs were no problem to my owls either. Though Mutt was no owl-lover himself, he wouldn't let any strange dog chase them—not without a fight.

Several times he saved Weeps from a mauling. But he didn't need to look after Wol.

There was a German shepherd who lived near us, and one day this dog met Wol out walking, and decided to see how horned owl tasted.

I heard the ruckus and came running. But by the time I got to the street Wol was sitting on the dog's back, digging his claws in for all he was worth, and ripping chunks out of the dog's ears with his beak. The shepherd headed down Spadina Avenue *yip-yip-yipping* till you could have heard it in Timbuctoo.

Wol rode him for three blocks, and might have ridden him right out of town if the dog hadn't dodged through a hole in a board fence and knocked Wol off. I had chased after them on my bike, but by the time I got to the fence Wol had picked himself up, given himself a shake or two to settle his feathers, and was his usual friendly self. He gave me a cheerful "Hoo-HOO-hoohoo!" and jumped up on the handle bars for a ride home.

Word seemed to get around after that, and the neighborhood dogs took to crossing over to the other side of the road when they saw Wol coming.

The Family Lupine

As a young man, Mowat was hired by the government to conduct a wolf study in the North. When he arrived in Churchill, he arranged to be flown to the Keewatin Barren Lands. There he made contact with a young trapper, Mike, who agreed to let Mowat use his cabin.

Spring had come to the Barrens with volcanic violence. The snows melted so fast that the frozen rivers could not carry the melted water, which flowed six feet deep on top of the ice. Finally the ice let go, with a thunderous explosion; then it promptly jammed, and in short order the river beside which I was living had entered into the cabin, bringing with it the accumulated refuse left by fourteen Huskies during a long winter.

Eventually the jam broke and the waters subsided; but the cabin had lost its charm, for the debris on the floor was a foot thick and somewhat repellent. I decided to pitch my tent on a gravel ridge above the cabin, and here I was vainly trying to go to sleep that evening when I became aware of unfamiliar sounds. Sitting bolt upright, I listened intently.

The sounds were coming from just across the river, to the north, and they were a weird medley of whines, whimpers, and small howls. My grip on the rifle slowly relaxed. The cries were obviously those of a Husky, probably a young one, and I deduced that it must be one of Mike's dogs (he owned three half-grown pups not yet trained to harness which ran loose after the team) that had got lost, retraced its way to the cabin, and was now begging for someone to come and be nice to it.

I was delighted. If that pup needed a friend, a chum, I was its man! I climbed hastily into my clothes, ran down to the riverbank, launched the canoe, and paddled lustily for the far bank.

The pup had never ceased its mournful plaint, and I was about to call out reassuringly when it occurred to me that an unfamiliar human voice might frighten it. I decided to stalk it instead, and to betray my presence only when I was close enough for soothing murmurs.

From the nature of the sounds I had assumed the dog was only a few yards away from the far bank, but as I made my way in the dim half-light, over broken boulders and across gravel ridges, the sounds seemed to remain at the same volume while I appeared to be getting no closer. I assumed the pup was retreating, perhaps out of shyness. In my anxiety not to startle it away entirely, I still kept quiet, even when the whimpering wail stopped, leaving me uncertain about the right direction to pursue. However, I saw a steep ridge looming ahead of me and I suspected that, once I gained its summit, I would have a clear enough view to enable me to locate the lost animal. As I neared the crest of the ridge I got down on my stomach (practicing the fieldcraft I had learned in the Boy Scouts) and cautiously inched my way the last few feet.

My head came slowly over the crest—and there was my quarry. He was lying down, evidently resting after his mournful singsong, and his nose was about six feet from mine. We stared at one another in silence. I do not know what went on in his massive skull, but my head was full of the most disturbing thoughts. I was peering straight into the amber gaze of a fully grown arctic wolf, who probably weighed more than I did, and who was certainly a lot better versed in close-combat techniques than I would ever be.

For some seconds neither of us moved but continued to stare hypnotically into one another's eyes. The wolf was the first to break the spell. With a spring which would have done justice to a Russian dancer, he leaped about a yard straight into the air and came down running. The textbooks say a wolf can run twenty-five miles an hour, but this one did not appear to be running, so much as flying low. Within seconds he had vanished from my sight.

My own reaction was not so dramatic, although I may very well have set some sort of a record for a cross-country traverse myself. My return over the river was accomplished with such verve that I paddled the canoe almost her full length up on the beach on the other side. Then, remembering my responsibilities to my scientific supplies, I entered the cabin, barred the door, and regardless of the discomfort caused by the stench of the debris on the floor made myself as comfortable as I could on top of the table for the balance of the short-lived night.

What with one thing and another I found it difficult to get to sleep. The table was too short and too hard; the atmosphere in the cabin was far too thick; and the memory of my recent encounter with the wolf was too vivid. I tried counting sheep, but they kept turning into wolves, leaving me more wakeful than ever. Finally, when some red-backed mice who lived under the floor began to produce noises which were realistic approximations of the sounds a wolf might make if he were snuffing at the door, I gave up all idea of sleep, lit Mike's oil lantern, and resigned myself to waiting for the dawn.

I allowed my thoughts to return to the events of the evening. Considering how brief the encounter with the wolf had been, I was amazed to discover the wealth of detail I could recall. In my mind's eye I could visualize the wolf as if I had known him (or her) for years. The image of that massive head with its broad white ruff, short pricked ears, tawny eyes, and grizzled muzzle was indelibly fixed in memory. So too was the image of the wolf in flight; the lean and sinewy motion and the overall impression of a beast the size of a small pony; an impression implicit with a feeling of lethal strength.

The more I thought about it, the more I realized that I had not cut a very courageous figure. My withdrawal from the scene had been hasty and devoid of dignity. But then the compensating thought occurred to me that the wolf had not stood upon the order of his (her) going either, and I began to feel somewhat better; a state of mind which may have been coincidental with the rising of the sun, which was now illuminating the bleak world outside my window with a gray and pallid light.

As the light grew stronger I even began to suspect that I had muffed an opportunity—one which might, moreover, never again recur. It was borne in upon me that I should have followed the wolf and endeavored to gain his confidence, or at least to convince him that I harbored no ill will toward his kind.

I undertook to clean up the Stygian mess in the cabin, and in the process I uncovered my compass. I set it on the windowsill while I continued with my work, but the sun caught its brass surface and it glittered at me so accusingly that I resigned myself to making another effort to restore the lost contact between me and the wolves.

My progress was slow, since I was carrying my rifle, shotgun, pistol and pistol belt, a small hatchet and my hunting knife, together with a flask of wolf-juice in case I fell into one of the icy streams.

It was a hot day, and spring days in the subarctic can be nearly as hot as in the tropics. The first mosquitoes were already heralding the approach of the sky-filling swarms which would soon make travel on the Barrens a veritable trip through hell. I located the wolf tracks and resolutely set out upon the trail.

It led directly across the muskeg for several miles; but although the wolf had sunk in only three or four inches, my steps sank in until I reached solid ice a foot beneath the surface. It was with great relief that I finally breasted another gravel ridge and lost all trace of the wolf tracks.

My attempts to find them again were perfunctory. As I gazed around me at the morose world of rolling muskeg and frost-shattered stone that stretched uninterruptedly to a horizon so distant it might as well have been the horizon of the sea, I felt lonelier than I had ever felt in all my life. No friendly sound of aircraft engines broke the silence of that empty sky. No distant rumble of traffic set the ground beneath my feet to shaking. Only the disembodied whistling of an unseen plover gave any indication that life existed anywhere in all this lunar land where no tree grew.

I found a niche amongst some lichen-covered rocks and, having firmly jammed myself into it, ate and drank my lunch. Then I picked up the binoculars and began to scan the barren landscape for some signs of life.

Directly in front of me was the ice-covered bay of a great lake, and on the far side of this bay was something which at least relieved the somber monochrome of the muskeg colorings. It was a yellow sand esker, rising to a height of fifty or sixty feet and winding sinuously away into the distance like a gigantic snake.

These barren land eskers are the inverted beds of long-vanished rivers which once flowed through and over the glaciers that, ten thousand years ago, covered the Keewatin Barrens to a depth of several thousand feet. When the ice melted, sandy riverbeds were deposited on the land below, where they now provide almost the sole visual relief in the bleak monotony of the tundra plains.

I gazed at this one with affection, studying it closely; and as I swept it with my glasses I saw something move. The distance was great, but the impression I had was of someone, just the other side of the esker crest, waving his arm above his head. Much excited, I stumbled to my feet and trotted along the ridge to its termination on the shore of the bay. I was then not more than three hundred yards from the esker and when I got my breath back I took another look through the glasses.

The object I had previously glimpsed was still in view, but now it looked like a white feather boa being vehemently waved by persons or person unseen. It was a most inexplicable object, and nothing I had ever heard of in my study of natural history seemed to fit it. As I stared in perplexity, the first boa was joined by a second one, also waving furiously, and both boas began to move slowly along, parallel to the crest of the esker.

I began to feel somewhat uneasy, for here was a phenomenon which did not seem to be subject to scientific explanation. In fact I was on the point of abandoning my interest in the spectacle until some expert in psychic research happened along—when, without warning, both boas turned toward me, began rising higher and higher, and finally revealed themselves as the tails of two wolves proceeding to top the esker.

The esker overlooked my position on the bay's shore, and I felt as nakedly exposed as the lady in the famous brassière advertisement. Hunkering down to make myself as small as possible, I wormed my way into the rocks and did my best to be unobtrusive. I need not have worried. The wolves paid no attention to me, if indeed they even saw me. They were far too engrossed in their own affairs, which, as I slowly and incredulously began to realize, were at that moment centered around the playing of a game of tag.

It was difficult to believe my eyes. They were romping like a pair of month-old pups! The smaller wolf (who soon gave concrete evidence that she was a female) took the initiative. Putting her head down on her forepaws and elevating her posterior in a most undignified manner, she suddenly pounced toward the much larger male whom I now recognized as my earlier acquaintance. He, in his attempt to evade her, tripped and went sprawling. Instantly she was upon him, nipping him smartly in the backside, before leaping away to run around him in frenzied circles. The male scrambled to his feet and gave chase, but only by the most strenuous efforts was he able to close the gap until he, in his turn, was able to nip *her* backside. Thereupon the roles were again reversed, and the female began to pursue the male, who led her on a wild scrabble up, over, down, and back across the esker until finally both wolves lost their footing on the steep slope and went skidding down it inextricably locked together.

When they reached the bottom they separated, shook the sand out of their hair, and stood panting heavily, almost nose to nose. Then the female reared up and quite literally embraced the male with both forepaws while she proceeded to smother him in long-tongued kisses.

The male appeared to be enduring this overt display of affection, rather than enjoying it. He kept trying to avert his head, to no avail. Nevertheless he bore it with what stoicism he could muster until the female tired. Turning from him, she climbed halfway up the esker slope and . . . disappeared.

She seemed to have vanished off the face of the earth without leaving a trace behind her. Not until I swung the glasses back toward a dark shadow in a fold of the esker near where I had last seen her did I understand. The dark shadow was the mouth of a cave, or den, and the female wolf had almost certainly gone into it.

I was so elated by the realization that I had not only located a pair of wolves, but by an incredible stroke of fortune had found their den as well, that I forgot all caution and ran to a nearby knoll in order to gain a better view of the den mouth.

The male wolf, who had been loafing about the foot of the esker after the departure of his wife, instantly saw me. In three or four bounds he reached the ridge of the esker, where he stood facing me in an attitude of tense and threatening vigilance. As I looked up at him my sense of exhilaration waned rapidly. He no longer seemed like a playful pup, but had metamorphosed into a magnificent engine of destruction which impressed me so much that the neck of my flask positively rattled against my teeth.

I decided I had better not disturb the wolf family any more that day, for fear of upsetting them and perhaps forcing them to move away. So I withdrew. It was not an easy withdrawal, for one of the most difficult things I know of is to walk backward up a broken rocky slope for three quarters of a mile encumbered, as I was, by the complex hardware of a scientist's trade.

When I reached the ridge from which I had first seen the wolves I took a last quick look through the binoculars. The female was still invisible, and the male had so far relaxed his attitude of vigilance as to lie down on the crest of the esker. While I watched he turned around two or three times, as a dog will, and then settled himself, nose under tail, with the evident intention of having a nap.

I was much relieved to see he was no longer interested in me, for it would have been a tragedy if my accidental intrusion had unduly disturbed these wolves, thereby prejudicing what promised to be a unique opportunity to study the beasts I had come so far to find.

I made a decision that I would go open-minded into the lupine world and learn to see and know the wolves, not for what they were supposed to be, but for what they actually were.

As I grew more completely attuned to their daily round of family life I found it increasingly difficult to maintain an impersonal attitude toward the wolves. No matter how hard I tried to regard them with scientific objectivity, I could not resist the impact of their individual personalities. Because he reminded me irresistibly of a Royal Gentleman for whom I worked as a simple soldier during the war, I found myself calling the father of the family George, even though in my notebooks he was austerely identified only as Wolf "A."

George was a massive and eminently regal beast whose coat was silver-white. He was about a third larger than his mate, but he hardly needed this extra bulk to emphasize his air of masterful certainty. George had presence. His dignity was unassailable, yet he was by no means aloof. Conscientious to a fault, thoughtful of others, and affectionate within reasonable bounds, he was the kind of father whose idealized image appears in many wistful books of human family reminiscences, but whose real prototype has seldom paced the earth upon two legs. George was, in brief, the kind of father every son longs to acknowledge as his own.

His wife was equally memorable. A slim, almost pure-white wolf with a thick ruff around her face, and wide-spaced, slightly slanted eyes, she seemed the picture of a minx. Beautiful, ebullient, passionate to a degree, and devilish when the mood was on her, she hardly looked like the epitome of motherhood; yet there could have been no better mother anywhere. I found myself calling her Angeline, although I have never been able to trace the origin of that name in the murky depths of my own subconscious. I respected and liked George very much, but I became deeply fond of Angeline, and still live in hopes that I can somewhere find a human female who embodies all her virtues.

Angeline and George seemed as devoted a mated pair as one could hope to find. As far as I could tell they never quarreled, and the delight with which they greeted each other after even a short absence was obviously unfeigned.

One factor concerning the organization of the family mystified me very much at first. During my early visit to the den I had seen *three* adult wolves; and during the first few days of observing the den I had again glimpsed the odd-wolf-out several times. He posed a major conundrum, for while I could accept the idea of a contented domestic group consisting of mated male and female and a bevy of pups, I had not yet progressed far enough into the wolf world to be able to explain, or to accept, the apparent existence of an eternal triangle.

Whoever the third wolf was, he was definitely a character. He was smaller than George, not so lithe and vigorous, and with a gray overcast to his otherwise white coat. He became "Uncle Albert" to me after the first time I saw him with the pups.

The sixth morning of my vigil had dawned bright and sunny, and Angeline and the pups took advantage of the good weather. Hardly was the sun risen (at 3 a.m.) when they all left the den and adjourned to a nearby sandy knoll. Here the pups worked over their mother with an enthusiasm which would certainly have driven any human female into hysterics. They were hungry; but they were also full to the ears with hellery. Two of them did their best to chew off Angeline's tail, worrying it and fighting over it until I thought I could actually see her fur flying like spindrift; while the other two did what they could to remove her ears.

Angeline stood it with noble stoicism for about an hour and then, sadly disheveled, she attempted to protect herself by sitting on her tail and tucking her mauled head down between her legs. This was a fruitless effort. The pups went for her feet, one to each paw, and I was treated to the spectacle of the demon killer of the wilds trying desperately to cover her paws, her tail, and her head at one and the same instant.

Eventually she gave it up. Harassed beyond endurance she leaped away from her brood and raced to the top of a high sand ridge behind the den. The four pups rolled cheerfully off in pursuit, but before they could reach her she gave vent to a most peculiar cry.

The whole question of wolf communications was to intrigue me more and more as time went on, but on this occasion I was still laboring under the delusion that complex communications among animals other than man did not exist. I could make nothing definite of Angeline's high-pitched and yearning whine-cum-howl. I did, however, detect a plaintive quality in it which made my sympathies go out to her.

I was not alone. Within seconds of her *cri de coeur*, and before the mob of pups could reach her, a savior appeared.

It was the third wolf. He had been sleeping in a bed hollowed in the sand at the southern end of the esker where it dipped down to disappear beneath the waters of the bay. I had not known he was there until I saw his head come up. He jumped to his feet, shook himself, and trotted straight toward the den—intercepting the pups as they prepared to scale the last slope to reach their mother.

I watched, fascinated, as he used his shoulder to bowl the leading pup over on its back and send it skidding down the lower slope toward the den. Having broken the charge, he then nipped another pup lightly on its fat behind; then he shepherded the lot of them back to what I later came to recognize as the playground area.

I hesitate to put human words into a wolf's mouth, but the effect of what followed was crystal clear. "If it's a workout you kids want," he might have said, "then I'm your wolf!"

And so he was. For the next hour he played with the pups with as much energy as if he were still one himself. The games were varied, but many of them were quite recognizable. Tag was the standby, and Albert was always "it." Leaping, rolling, and weaving amongst the pups, he never left the area of the nursery knoll, while at the same time leading the youngsters such a chase that they eventually gave up.

Albert looked them over for a moment and then, after a quick glance toward the crest where Angeline was now lying in a state of peaceful relaxation, he flung himself in among the tired pups, sprawled on his back, and invited mayhem. They were game. One by one they roused and went into battle. They were really roused this time, and no holds were barred—by them, at any rate.

Some of them tried to choke the life out of Albert, although their small teeth, sharp as they were, could never have penetrated his heavy ruff. One of them, in an excess of infantile sadism, turned its back on him and pawed a shower of sand into his face. The others took to leaping as high into the air as their bowed little legs would propel them; coming down with a satisfying thump on Albert's vulnerable belly. In between jumps they tried to chew the life out of whatever vulnerable parts came to tooth.

I began to wonder how much he could stand. Evidently he could stand a lot, for not until the pups were totally exhausted and had collapsed into complete somnolence did he get to his feet, careful not to step on the small, sprawled forms, and disengage himself. Even then he did not return to the comfort of his own bed (which he had undoubtedly earned after a night of hard hunting) but settled himself instead on the edge of the nursery knoll, where he began wolf-napping, taking a quick look at the pups every few minutes to make sure they were still safely near at hand.

His true relationship to the rest of the family was still uncertain; but as far as I was concerned he had become, and would remain, "good old Uncle Albert."

[One June evening] I was alone at the tent when the wolves gathered for their pre-hunt ritual singsong, but a few hours later a driving rain began and I had to give up my observations.

There were no wolves in sight the next morning when the rain ceased, the mist lifted, and I could again begin observing; but shortly before nine o'clock George and Uncle Albert appeared on the crest of the esker.

Both seemed nervous, or at least uneasy. After a good deal of restless pacing, nose sniffing, and short periods of immobility during which they stared intently over the surrounding landscape, they split up. George took himself off to the highest point of the esker, where he sat down in full view and began to scan the country to the east and south. Uncle Albert trotted off along the ridge to the north, and lay down on a rocky knoll, staring out over the western plains.

There was no sign of Angeline, and this, together with the unusual actions of the male wolves, began to make me uneasy too. The thought that something might have happened to Angeline struck me with surprising pain. I had not realized how fond I was becoming of her, but now that she appeared to be missing I began to worry about her in dead earnest.

I was on the point of leaving my tent and climbing the ridge to have a look for her myself, when she forestalled me. As I took a last quick glance through the telescope I saw her emerge from the den—with something in her mouth—and start briskly across the face of the esker. For a moment I could not make out what it was she was carrying, then with a start of surprise I recognized it as one of the pups.

Making good time despite her burden—the pup must have weighed ten or fifteen pounds—she trotted diagonally up the esker slope and disappeared into a small stand of spruce. Fifteen minutes later she was back at the den for another pup, and by ten o'clock she had moved the last of them.

After she disappeared for the final time both male wolves gave up their vigils—they had evidently been keeping guard over the move—and followed her, leaving me to stare bleakly over an empty landscape. I was greatly perturbed. The only explanation which I could think of for this mass exodus was that I had somehow disturbed the wolves so seriously they had felt impelled to abandon their den. If this was indeed the case, I knew I would only make matters worse by trying to follow them. Not being able to think of anything else to do, I hurried back to the cabin to consult Ootek.*

The Eskimo immediately set my fears at rest. He explained that this shifting of the pups was a normal occurrence with every wolf family at about this time of year. There were several reasons for it, so he told me. In the first place the pups had now been weaned, and, since there was no water supply near the den, it was necessary to move them to a location where they could slack their thirst elsewhere than at their mother's teats. Secondly, the pups were growing too big for the den, which now could barely contain them all. Thirdly, and perhaps most important, it was time for the youngsters to give up babyhood and begin their education.

"They are too old to live in a hole in the ground, but still too young to follow their parents," Mike interpreted, as Ootek explained. "So the old wolves take them to a new place where there is room for the pups to move around and to learn about the world, but where they are still safe."

As it happened both Ootek and Mike were familiar with the location of the new "summer den," and the next day we moved the observation tent to a position partly overlooking it.

The pups' new home, half a mile from the old den, was a narrow, truncated ravine filled with gigantic boulders which had been split off the cliff walls by frost action. A small stream ran through it. It also embraced an area of grassy marsh which was alive with meadow mice: an ideal place for the pups to learn the first principles of hunting. Exit to and entry from the ravine involved a stiff climb, which was too much for the youngsters, so that they could be left in their new home with little danger of their straying; and since they were now big enough to hold their own with the only other local carnivores of any stature—the foxes and hawks—they had nothing to fear.

---

* A relative of Mike's.

For the rest of the summer, Mowat reveled in observing the wolves. But as autumn approached, he realized he would soon be leaving the Barrens.

In order to round out my study of wolf family life, I needed to know what the den was like inside—how deep it was, the diameter of the passage, the presence (if any) of a nest at the end of the burrow, and such related information. For obvious reasons I had not been able to make this investigation while the den was occupied, and since that time I had been too busy with other work to get around to it. Now, with time running out, I was in a hurry.

I trotted across-country toward the den and I was within half-a-mile of it when there was a thunderous roar behind me. It was so loud and unexpected that I involuntarily flung myself down on the moss. The Norseman came over at about fifty feet. As it roared past, the plane waggled its wings gaily in salute, then lifted to skim the crest of the wolf esker, sending a blast of sand down the slope with its propeller wash. I picked myself up and quieted my thumping heart, thinking black thoughts about the humorist in the now rapidly vanishing aircraft.

The den ridge was, as I had expected (and as the Norseman would have made quite certain in any case), wolfless. Reaching the entrance to the burrow I shed my heavy trousers, tunic and sweater, and taking a flashlight (whose batteries were very nearly dead) and measuring-tape from my pack, I began the difficult task of wiggling down the entrance tunnel.

The flashlight was so dim it cast only an orange glow—barely sufficient to enable me to read the marks on the measuring-tape. I squirmed onward, descending at a forty-five-degree angle, for about eight feet. My mouth and eyes were soon full of sand and I was beginning to suffer from claustrophobia, for the tunnel was just big enough to admit me.

At the eight-foot mark the tunnel took a sharp upward bend and swung to the left. I pointed the torch in the new direction and pressed the switch.

Four green lights in the murk ahead reflected back the dim torch beam.

In this case green was not my signal to advance. I froze where I was, while my startled brain tried to digest the information that at least two wolves were with me in the den.

Despite my close familiarity with the wolf family, this was the kind of situation where irrational but deeply ingrained prejudices completely over-master reason and experience. To be honest, I was so frightened that paralysis gripped me. I had no weapon of any sort, and in my awkward posture I could barely have gotten one hand free with which to ward off an attack. It seemed inevitable that the wolves *would* attack me, for even a gopher will make a fierce defense when he is cornered in his den.

The wolves did not even growl.

Save for the two faintly glowing pairs of eyes, they might not have been there at all.

The paralysis began to ease and, though it was a cold day, sweat broke out all over my body. In a fit of blind bravado, I shoved the torch forward as far as my arm would reach.

It gave just sufficient light for me to recognize Angeline and one of the pups. They were scrunched hard against the back wall of the den; and they were as motionless as death.

The shock was wearing off by this time, and the instinct for self-preservation was regaining command. As quickly as I could I began wiggling back up the slanting tunnel, tense with the expectation that at any instant the wolves would charge. But by the time I reached the entrance and had scrambled well clear of it, I had still not heard nor seen the slightest sign of movement from the wolves.

I sat down on a stone and shakily lit a cigarette, becoming aware as I did so that I was no longer frightened. Instead an irrational rage possessed me. If I had had my rifle I believe I might have reacted in brute fury and tried to kill both wolves.

The cigarette burned down, and a wind began to blow out of the somber northern skies. I began to shiver again; this time from cold instead of rage. My anger was passing and I was limp in the aftermath. Mine had been the fury of resentment born of fear: resentment against the beasts who had engendered naked terror in me and who, by so doing, had intolerably affronted my human ego.

I was appalled at the realization of how easily I had forgotten, and how readily I had denied, all that the summer sojourn with the wolves had taught me about them…and about myself. I thought of Angeline and her pup cowering at the bottom of the den where they had taken refuge from the thundering apparition of the aircraft, and I was shamed.

Somewhere to the eastward a wolf howled; lightly, questioningly. I knew the voice, for I had heard it many times before. It was George, sounding the wasteland for an echo from the missing members of his family. But for me it was a voice which spoke of the lost world which once was ours before we chose the alien role; a world which I had glimpsed and almost entered…only to be excluded, at the end, by my own self.

The Whale

Mowat lived in Burgeo, Newfoundland, for eight years. During that time, he and his wife Claire took an extended trip to Europe and the Soviet Union. Happy to be home, they were not prepared for some unsettling news.

During my years in Burgeo I had been called upon on a number of occasions to speak, or write, on behalf of individuals and groups who felt themselves incapable of reaching the ears of those in authority. Although a little vague about the real nature of my work as a writer, they assumed I had some kind of influence with those up above.

After supper on Thursday two fishermen from Smalls Island walked into our kitchen bearing gifts of cod tongues and a huge slab of halibut. They sat on the day bed and we talked for a while about the state of the fishery, the weather, and other usual topics of Burgeo life. It was not until they were leaving that the real reason for the visit came out.

"I suppose, Skipper, you knows about the whale? The one down in Aldridges Pond. Big feller. Been in there quite a time."

"What the devil would a whale be doing in there?" I asked incredulously. "What kind of a whale is it?"

He was vague. "Don't rightly know. Black, like; with a girt big fin. They says it can't get clear... Well, goodnight to you, Missus, Skipper."

And with that they vanished.

My curiosity was aroused.

Sim Spencer was alone in his little store, laboriously working up his accounts. Rather reluctantly, it seemed to me, he admitted to having heard something about the Aldridges whale. When I asked him why he hadn't told me before, knowing how interested I was in anything to do with whales, he was embarrassed.

"Well," he said, fumbling for words. "They's been a lot of foolishness... a shame what some folks does... wouldn't want to bother you with the likes of that... but now as you knows, I thinks 'tis just as well."

The implications of this escaped me at the time, but soon became clear enough. The reason I had not been told about the whale was that many of the people were ashamed of what was happening and did not want to talk about it with outsiders; and even after five years I was still something of a newcomer in their midst.

Sim took me to see the Hanns. They were reticent at first but they did describe the whale in fair detail; and I now realized there was an excellent if almost unbelievable chance it might turn out to be one of the great rorquals. Having seen Aldridges Pond in the past, I knew it to be an almost perfect natural aquarium, quite large enough to contain even a Blue Whale in some kind of comfort.

The prospect that, for the first time in history, so far as I knew, it might be possible to come to close quarters with the mystery of one of the mighty lords of Ocean, was wildly exciting. I was in such a hurry to rush home and tell Claire about it that Kenneth Hann's concluding words did not quite sink in.

"They says," he warned, "some fellers been shooting at it. It could get hurted, Skipper, an' they keeps it up."

Probably some damn fool has been taking pot shots at it with a .22, I thought, and put the warning out of mind. As I hurried across Messers bridge in the gathering darkness, my thoughts were fixed on tomorrow, and my imagination was beginning to run away as I contemplated what could happen if the trapped whale indeed turned out to be one of the giants of the seas.

Early next morning I telephoned Danny Green, a lean, sardonic, and highly intelligent man in his middle thirties who had been the high-lining skipper of a dragger but had given that up to become skipper, mate, and crew of the little Royal Canadian Mounted Police motor launch. Danny not only knew—and was happy to comment on—everything of importance that happened on the Sou'west Coast, he was also familiar with and interested in whales. What he had to tell me brought my excitement to fever pitch.

"I'm pretty sure 'tis one of the big ones, Farley. Can't say what kind. Haven't seen it meself but it might be a Humpback, a Finner, or even a Sulphur." He paused a moment. "What's left of it. The sports have been blasting hell out of it this past week."

As Danny gave me further details of how local people had been shooting at and wounding the whale, I was at first appalled, then furious.

"Are they bloody well crazy? This is a chance in a million. If that whale lives, Burgeo'll be famous all over the world. *Shooting* at it! What the hell's the matter with the constable?"

Danny explained that our one policeman was a temporary replacement for the regular constable, who was away on leave. The new man, Constable Murdoch, was from New Brunswick. He knew nothing about Burgeo and not much about Newfoundland. He was hesitant to interfere in local matters unless he received an official complaint.

At my request, Danny put him on the phone.

"Whoever's doing that shooting is breaking the game laws, you know," I told him. "It's forbidden to take rifles into the country. Can't you put a stop to it?"

Murdoch was apologetic and cooperative. Not only did he undertake to investigate the shooting, he offered to make a patrol to Aldridges Pond and take me with him. However, Claire and I had already made other arrangements with two Messers fishermen, Curt Bungay and Wash Pink, who fished together in Curt's new boat. They were an oddly assorted pair. Young, and newly married, Curt was one of those people about whom the single adjective, "round," says it all. His crimson-hued face was a perfect circle, with round blue eyes, a round little nose, and a circular mouth. Although he was not fat, his body was a cylinder supported on legs as round and heavy as mill logs. Wash Pink was almost the complete opposite. A much older man, who had known hard times in a distant outport, he was lean, desiccated, and angular. And whereas Curt was a born talker and story teller, Wash seldom opened his mouth except in moments of singular stress.

A few minutes after talking to Murdoch, Claire and I were under way in Curt's longliner. I was dithering between hope that we would find a great whale in the Pond, alive and well, and the possibility that it might have escaped or, even worse, have succumbed to the shooting. Claire kept her usual cool head, as her notes testify:

"It was blowing about 40 miles an hour from the northwest," she wrote, "and I hesitated to go along. But Farley said I would regret it all my life if I didn't. Burgeo being Burgeo, it wouldn't have surprised me if the 'giant whale' had turned out to be a porpoise. It was rough and icy cold crossing Short Reach but we got to Aldridges all right and sidled cautiously through the narrow channel. It was several hours from high tide and there was only five feet of water, which made Curt very nervous for the safety of his brand-new boat.

"We slid into the pretty little Pond under a dash of watery sunlight. It was a beautifully protected natural harbor ringed with rocky cliffs that ran up to the 300-foot crest of Richards Head. Little clumps of dwarfed black spruce clung in the hollows here and there along the shore.

"There was nobody and nothing to be seen except a few gulls soaring high overhead. We looked eagerly for signs of the whale, half expecting it to come charging out of nowhere and send us scurrying for the exit. There was no sign of it and I personally concluded it had left—if it had ever been in the Pond at all.

"I was ready to go below and try to get warm when somebody cried out that they saw something. We all looked and saw a long, black shape that looked like a giant sea-serpent, curving quietly out of the water, and slipping along from head to fin, and then down again and out of sight.

"We just stared, speechless and unbelieving, at this vast monster. Then there was a frenzy of talk.

"'It's a *whale* of a whale!... Must be fifty, sixty feet long!... That's no Pothead, not that one...'

"Indeed, it was no Pothead but an utterly immense, solitary and lonely monster, trapped, Heaven knew how, in this rocky prison.

"We chugged to the middle of the Pond just as the R.C.M.P. launch entered and headed for us. Farley called to Danny Green and they agreed to anchor the two boats in deep water near the south end of the Pond and stop the engines.

"Then began a long, long watch during which the hours went by like minutes. It was endlessly fascinating to watch the almost serpentine coming and going of this huge beast. It would surface about every four or five minutes as it followed a circular path around and around the Pond. At first the circles took it well away from us but as time passed, and everyone kept perfectly still, the circles narrowed, coming closer and closer to the boats.

"Twice the immense head came lunging out of the water high into the air. It was as big as a small house, glistening black on top and fish-white underneath. Then down would go the nose, and the blowhole would break surface, and then the long, broad back, looking like the bottom of an overturned ship, would slip into our sight. Finally the fin would appear, at least four feet tall, and then a boiling up of water from the flukes and the whale was gone again.

"Farley identified it as a Fin Whale, the second largest animal ever to live on earth. We could see the marks of bullets—holes and slashes—across the back from the blowhole to the fin. It was just beyond me to even begin to understand the mentality of men who would amuse themselves filling such a majestic creature full of bullets. Why *try* to kill it? There is no mink or fox farm here to use the meat. None of the people would eat it. No, there is no motive of food or profit; only a lust to kill. But then I wonder, is it any different than the killer's lust that makes the mainland sportsmen go out in their big cars to slaughter rabbits or ground-hogs? It just seems so much more terrible to kill a whale!

"We could trace its progress even under water by the smooth, swirling tide

its flukes left behind. It appeared to be swimming only about six feet deep and it kept getting closer to us so we began to catch glimpses of it under the surface, its white underparts appearing pale aqua-green against the darker background of deep water.

"The undulations on the surface came closer and closer until the whale was surfacing within twenty feet of the boats. It seemed to deliberately look at us from time to time as if trying to decide whether we were dangerous. Oddly, the thought never crossed my mind that *it* might be dangerous to us. Later on I asked some of the others if they had been afraid of this, the mightiest animal any of us was ever likely to meet in all our lives, and nobody had felt any fear at all. We were too enthralled to be afraid.

"Apparently the whale decided we were not dangerous. It made another sweep and this time that mighty head passed right under the Mountie's boat. They pointed and waved and we stared down too. Along came the head, like a submarine, but much more beautiful, slipping along under us no more than six feet away. Just then Danny shouted: 'Here's his tail! Here's his tail!'

"The tail was just passing under the police launch while the head was under *our* boat, and the two boats were a good seventy feet apart! The flippers, each as long as a dory, showed green beneath us, then the whole unbelievable length of the body flowed under the boat, silently, with just a faint slick swirl of water on the surface from the flukes. It was almost impossible to believe what we were seeing! This incredibly vast being, perhaps eighty tons in weight, so Farley guessed, swimming below us with the ease and smoothness of a salmon.

"Danny told me later the whale could have smashed up both our boats as easily as we would smash a couple of eggs. Considering what people had done to it, why didn't it take revenge? Or is it only mankind that takes revenge?"

Once she accepted the fact that our presence boded her no harm, the whale showed a strange interest in us, almost as if she took pleasure in being close to our two 40-foot boats, whose undersides may have looked faintly whale-like in shape. Not only did she pass directly under us several times but she also passed between the two boats, carefully threading her way between our anchor cables. We had the distinct impression she was lonely—an impression shared by the Hann brothers when she hung close to their small boat. Claire went so far as to suggest the whale was seeking help, but how could we know about that?

I was greatly concerned about the effects of the gunning but, apart from a multitude of bullet holes, none of which showed signs of bleeding, she appeared to be in good health. Her movements were sure and powerful and there was no bloody discoloration in her blow. Because I so much wished to believe it, I concluded that the bullets had done no more than superficial damage and that, with luck, the great animal would be none the worse for her ordeal by fire.

At dusk we reluctantly left the Pond. Our communion with the whale had left all of us half hypnotized. We had almost nothing to say to each other until the R.C.M.P. launch pulled alongside and Constable Murdoch shouted:

"There'll be no more shooting. I guarantee you that. Danny and me'll patrol every day from now on, and twice a day if we have to."

Murdoch's words brought me my first definite awareness of a decision which I must already have arrived at below—or perhaps above—the limited levels of conscious thought. As we headed back to Messers, I knew I was committed to the saving of that whale, as passionately as I had ever been committed to anything in my life. I still do not know why I felt such an instantaneous compulsion. Later it was possible to think of a dozen reasons, but these were afterthoughts—not reasons at the time. If I were a mystic, I might explain it by saying I had heard a call, and that may not be such a mad explanation after all.

Peter and the Birds

In his early days as a writer, Mowat returned to Europe to visit in peacetime places he had known only as battlefields in the Second World War. With his first wife, Frances, he ended the trip in Britain. Their friends Harold and Maureen Shortt had a treat in store for them.

Although our time abroad was drawing to an end, the Shortts weren't yet finished with us.

"You've seen a deal of what went on in these parts in the dim and distant," said Harold one evening at the Swan. "Maureen and I think you ought to see another side before you flit. One that ought to be to your taste. We'd like to take you down to Slimbridge tomorrow to visit Peter Scott."

"Peter Scott? Son of the Antarctic explorer?"

"Aye, that's the lad. Different breed from his old dad, but he does big things too."

We were away at eight, after Sarah Cooper had stuffed Fran and me with porridge and clotted cream, and scrambled eggs accompanied by fried kidneys, sausages, and tomatoes. As we waddled out the door of the Swan, Sar thrust a bulging sack upon us. In response to a questioning glance from me, she smiled and said, "Gie un to Harold. He'll find a use for un."

Harold and Maureen were waiting in their sedate old Ford Pilot. They drove us by way of Dursley, sprawled in the bottom of its own valley a mile from Uley.

Harold turned west towards the Severn. Soon we were wobbling along a dirt track across a vast, rain-sodden, estuarine plain on which stood the hamlet of Slimbridge. Its half-dozen gray stone buildings seemed mired in time and far lonelier than any cloud. Beyond it a seemingly endless salt marsh swept to the muddy tidal flats of the Severn. This was Peter Scott's domain.

Born in 1909, Peter had been only four years old when his famous father, Robert Falcon Scott, perished while returning from his epic journey to the South Pole. During his childhood Peter had found himself isolated from his contemporaries by the towering presence of a dead hero. As I myself had done in my time, Peter turned to the world of birds, especially waterfowl, seeking companionship and solace. By the time he was twenty-nine, he had become well known for his haunting paintings of ducks, geese, and swans.

Then the war came. He served through it with the Royal Navy, mostly in the "little ships"—motor torpedo boats, mine sweepers, and the like—where he encountered his fair share of death and destruction.

Although an avid hunter before the war, Peter wanted no more of killing after it. In 1946 he leased twenty acres of prime waterfowling ground from the Berkeley estate, whose lords had used the vast salt marshes called the Dumbles as a private hunting preserve through five centuries. On this little patch of sodden land, Peter set himself to the task of saving what he could of an avian world that had been decimated, not by the guns of war but by the guns of "sportsmen." Here he founded a sanctuary called the Severn Wild Fowl Trust, unique in its time and still an extraordinary venture.

At the time of our visit, Peter was living with his wife and son in a farm worker's cottage crammed with his books and paintings. The family was at breakfast when Harold knocked on their door. The Scotts could hardly have been pleased to see visitors at such an hour, but when Peter heard my name he thought a moment, then shook my hand warmly, and invited us in.

"I've got your book, you know. I was in your part of the Arctic just two years after you. A bit farther north—on the Perry River—looking for Ross's geese. John Ingebritson at Churchill told me about your penchant for running around with wolves. I'm afraid we've no wolves here, but welcome to the Trust."

Peter had a high-domed forehead, receding hairline, and an engaging smile. While his wife poured tea, I told him something about our journey, now almost concluded.

"Jolly good thing you came along here before you went off home. You know about birds, and how badly things are going for a lot of them—especially the waterfowl. So it'll be a delight to show you what we're trying to do about it."

He took us first to the so-called Big Pen, an acre of meadow enclosed by a waist-high wire mesh fence. It was aquiver with all sizes, colors, and shapes of waterfowl. Now I discovered that the bag Sarah had sent along was stuffed with bread crusts and cake crumbs. When Harold instructed Fran and me to dispense largesse from it, we were mobbed by hundreds of swans, geese, and ducks yanking at our clothing with their beaks, flapping their wings, quacking, honking, and hissing. It was a bit like Alfred Hitchcock's eerie film, *The Birds*, except that it had no ominous overtones.

Most of these birds were exceedingly gentle even while taking food from our hands. The exception was an Egyptian gander who seized my fingers in his horny beak and would not let go. There ensued a tug-of-war that I lost on points. Peter was amused.

"Nasty chap, that one. Don't bend over or he'll go for your nose."

An Emperor goose crowded in behind Fran and vainly tried to get her attention by nibbling the hem of her skirt. When that failed the goose thrust her head and neck under the skirt, eliciting an instant response.

I was impressed by the avian display around us, but a little disapproving too, for I do not hold with keeping wild animals in captivity.

"It'd be better," I said in Fran's ear, "if all these birds were free to go where they pleased."

Peter overheard me. "Oh, but they *are*," he cried indignantly. "Look there!" He pointed towards the river flats where flight after flight of geese and ducks were rising and heading in our direction. Soon the air was throbbing and whistling with the sound of wings as flock after flock pitched into the mob surrounding us, anxious not to be too late for their "elevenses," as Maureen put it.

Leaving Maureen and Harold to deal with the swelling multitudes, Peter led Fran and me off to one side where we could hear ourselves think.

"There are about forty-odd species in the Big Pen at this moment," he told us. "Some are native to Britain, but most are rare types brought here from all over the world. And most *are* free to come and go as they please. Only the really endangered ones are pinioned, to make sure they don't come to any grief."

Peter himself had originally doubted the wisdom of allowing the foreign birds their freedom. Time reassured him. There had been only one serious "break" and it was unintentional.

A flock of snow geese, the nucleus of which Scott had brought back from arctic Canada, was in the habit of making a morning exercise flight over the Severn estuary. One January in 1952 a heavy fog swept in while the birds were aloft and they got lost.

The English being the nature lovers they are, a nationwide search ensued. The BBC broadcast special alerts. Bird watchers sallied out in their hundreds. Peter chartered a plane and flew up and down the coast, hoping to find the flock and shepherd it back to the Dumbles. A lone bird was reported a hundred miles to the north, wearily slogging its way on foot across a farmer's field. Others were seen in remote parts of the British Isles, but only half a dozen found their own way home. Peter thought the rest had probably been shot.

Those who returned were so shaken by the experience of life in the raw that thereafter they took to the air only on clear days and for brief periods.

I asked Peter if there had been much trouble with poachers.

"Not really. What I've done, you see, is give every known or suspected poacher for miles and miles around special warden membership in the Trust." He smiled. "Works like a charm. It'd be as much as a man's life was worth to take a shot at one of our birds now."

That happy breed of killers who call themselves sportsmen would have found the targets massed before us irresistible. The variety alone would have made them drool. In the milling mobs around Harold and Maureen, I could pick out black swans from Australia, trumpeter swans from Canada, Sushkin's geese from Siberia, half a dozen species of European geese, Bahamian pintails, Chilean teal, Abyssinian yellowbills, African pollards, New Zealand scaup, Brazilian teal, Magellan geese, and other species, as they say, too numerous to mention.

If the variety of world rarities would have driven a sport hunter half insane, the numbers would have ensured dementia. Although it was summer, between two and three thousand geese and about twice as many ducks remained in the vicinity of the sanctuary, spreading out over the Dumbles to feed and breed. In winter, Peter told us, as many as ten thousand northern geese, mainly graylag, pink-footed, and white-fronted, ended their southerly migration flight on the Dumbles, where they remained until spring sent them back to Iceland and Greenland to raise new families.

Peter had begun his work with a lease on the land and not much else. His own small collection of live ducks and geese had vanished during the war years. He had no funds. But, as it turned out, he did have the support of a great many people who also realized that the sonorous voices crying on high in autumnal nights; the rush of wings over the marshes of the world; the kaleidoscopic play of living grace and color on lakes, rivers, and ponds were fast fading away. These people rallied around him to organize the Severn Wild Fowl Trust. Founding members included Field Marshal Viscount Alanbrooke, His Excellency Ahmen Aboud Pasha, half a dozen lords of the realm, and, most important, several thousand ordinary Britons.

Help came from unexpected quarters. When the holding and breeding pens were being built, paths laid, and ponds dug, much of the labor was provided gratis by German prisoners of war who were awaiting repatriation in a nearby camp. They volunteered almost en masse.

"It was a jolly queer sight, you know; all those *Kriegsmarine*, *Luftwaffe*, and *Wehrmacht* types rousting about in the mud, singing and larking like schoolboys to help a lot of birds. Why? I really can't say. We couldn't pay them anything. The foreman—he was a former paratrooper—told me once that just having a flock of graylags spiral down around him as if he was an old chum made him feel life might still be worth the living. He wanted to stay on permanently, but the authorities wouldn't let him."

As is all too often the case, the authorities gave Scott a lot of trouble. The hunting-shooting lobby in England wields great power, as indeed it does in every well-to-do country. It did not like Scott's application for the establishment of a no-hunting zone that would embrace much of the Dumbles. The lobby feared Scott would establish a dangerous precedent. Had the public not rallied strongly to his cause and won the day, the Trust would have found itself largely limited to rearing living targets for gunners, a fate that has overtaken all too many waterfowl "sanctuaries" in North America.

Then there was the Royal Air Force, which had several airfields in the region. In 1949 the RAF decided the Dumbles would make an excellent bombing and rocket-firing range. Expropriation proceedings were begun and would have succeeded had not the public become militantly aroused on behalf of Peter and the birds. Seldom defeated in the air, the RAF had to accept defeat on the ground. It did so with such bad grace that, when we were there, pilots of screaming jets were still going out of their way to "strafe" the geese.

"The odd thing is," said Peter with a grin, "the geese seem to know they've got the upper hand. I've often seen them casually break away in front of a jet like a bunch of children enjoying an exciting game. Or they'll sit unruffled on the flats and cackle with glee when a pilot diving on them has to pull up before he goes into the drink."

In the beginning the sanctuary harbored only about fifty waterfowl of ten species. By the end of the first year it held seventy different kinds. As word of Scott's intention to provide a breeding refuge for threatened species got around, a swelling stream of rare and endangered birds began arriving at Slimbridge. By 1952 the stream of refugees had become a feathered torrent flowing from every quarter of the globe, bringing such diverse creatures as flightless Steamer ducks from Tierra del Fuego; harlequin ducks from Labrador, pygmy geese from India, Koloa ducks from Hawaii, and Ross's geese from arctic Canada.

The most immediately threatened species constituted Peter's chief concern. These he set about rearing in the relative freedom, but security, of the sanctuary. He had two goals in mind. The first was to build a stock that would be large enough to ensure against total extinction if the species should disappear in the wild. The second was to rear additional birds to reinforce the wild stock in home territories where the species had been badly depleted.

Keeping the 130 different kinds of waterfowl gathered together at Slimbridge fed and in good health was a tremendous task, most of which fell on the shoulders of a young man named Sam Johnston. Young fish-eating ducks, for example, had to be started on a diet of maggots raised in the Trust's very own maggot factory. Older fish-eaters required vast quantities of small eels, sprats, and herring. Geese, fortunately, are mostly grass-eaters; but some geese and many sea ducks need marine plants, which Johnston and a crew of volunteers harvested in the estuary from a rickety old rowboat.

Another of Johnston's problems was keeping the various species of birds sorted out. Native waterfowl from all over Europe frequently dropped in, and some concluded this was the life for them and stayed for good. Some very rare birds, such as a Bewick's swan, arrived in this manner. These freeloaders, as Peter called them, sometimes mate with exotics from afar. The offspring quite literally look like nothing on earth. Weirdly marked hybrids wander happily about the pens and fly over the salt flats, making the job of record-keeping exceedingly difficult and giving amateur ornithologists conniptions. However, anything with wings was welcome at Slimbridge.

"I expect some scientists don't quite approve of how we do things," Peter apologized, "because, you see, we believe in everything being left as natural as possible. We try not to interfere more than we absolutely have to. Birds are like us, you know. If they feel at ease they do well. Otherwise they can go all to pieces."

He told us a story to illustrate this. Egyptian geese tend to be troublemakers so it was decided to send all except one gander away to a waterfowl park in Hampshire. The deprived gander thereupon fell madly in love with Johnston.

"It's the same nasty old bird that bit your hand. Used to follow poor Sam everywhere, trying to mate with him. Simply wouldn't take no for an answer. Poor chap was black-and-blue from fighting off the gander's advances. Then Sam got a bright idea. He shut the bird up in a shed with a German shepherd someone had given us for a watchdog . . . something we surely didn't need, not with several thousand geese about the place.

"Then, you see, the gander switched his affections to the dog. When Sam let them out, the poor shepherd was driven quite demented. Finally went to ground under the viewing stand where visitors go to watch the birds. Wouldn't come out at all. Just lay under there and howled as if his heart was breaking. Clearly either the gander or the dog had to go, and since the dog had no feathers, of course he was the one. We did find him a good home with an old chap in the village who can't abide birds. They get along famously, I'm told."

Peter and I got along famously too. Fran and the Shortts began to complain of hunger pangs and while they retired to the nearest pub for a bite of lunch, Peter took me for a walking tour of the Dumbles.

It carried me back to boyhood hikes looking for birds on the Saskatchewan prairie. Ducks and geese had still been abundant in those days but I had never expected to see them again in comparable numbers and variety. Walking (and wading) the Dumbles with Scott was like returning to another time. I did not keep count, but I am sure we saw a dozen kinds of geese and swans, and twice that many kinds of ducks.

All were fearless of us. Once when we perched on the edge of a seawall for a rest, a small flock of graylags came streaming across the estuary, saw us, veered abruptly, and pitched into the salt grass within arm's length. Straining their necks, they gurgled at us pleadingly.

"Young ganders," Peter apologized. "Should have gone off to Iceland in the spring with the rest of their lot. Now they seem to think it's up to me to find mates for them."

Farther along was a concrete pillbox built during the war to house a machine gun, as part of Britain's coastal defences. Peter had converted it into an observation blind. We spent an hour in it munching apples he pulled from a jacket pocket, smoking our pipes, and enjoying the show the birds were staging over the salt marshes and tidal flats.

The thought came to me that, although the need for sanctuary may be more immediate and urgent for some than for others, *all* creatures need it at some juncture in their lives. *All* creatures, including us.

I wanted to put the thought into words but felt awkward about doing so. Instead, I chose to remark on the concrete box through whose gun embrasures we were watching the birds.

"Hell of a good idea, this. Turning the sword into the plowshare, as it were."

Peter nodded. "Wouldn't it be grand to do the same with all the military hardware in the world?"

"Too bloody true! Only I'm afraid that isn't going to happen."

As if to emphasize the point, three Meteor jet fighters shrieked low overhead. I flinched, but the ducks and geese on the Dumbles paid no heed. They were in sanctuary.

A pair of lapwings mewed past, flapping their wings like giant bats. Peter watched them intently.

"P'raps you're right. It may *not* come to pass...but you know, Mowat, if it doesn't...and if we don't stop mucking things up other ways as well...one day the old Proprietor up in the sky is going to shout: 'Time, gentlemen!' and turn the lot of us out into the night."

His voice sank almost to a whisper, taking on the cadence of a childhood verse.

"And where will we go then, poor things?... And where will we go then?..."

Adventures

On the Water

Although our sojourn on the Saskatchewan plains satisfied my father in most respects, he nevertheless knew one hunger that the west could not still.

Before coming to Saskatoon he had always lived close to the open waters of the Great Lakes, and had been a sailor on them since his earliest days. Nor is this purely a figurative statement, for by his own account he was conceived on the placid waters of the Bay of Quinte—in a green canoe. He came by his passion for the water honestly.

During his first year in Saskatoon, he was able to stifle his nautical cravings beneath the weight of the many new experiences the west had to offer him; but during the long winter of the second prairie year, he began to dream. When he sat down to dinner of an evening he would be with Mother and myself in the flesh only, for in spirit he was dining on hardtack and salt beef on one of Nelson's ships. He took to carrying a piece of marlin in his pocket, and visitors to his office in the library would watch curiously as he tied and untied a variety of sailors' knots while talking in an abstracted voice about the problems of book distribution in prairie towns.

Knowing my father, and knowing too that he was not the kind to remain satisfied with a dream world, it came as no surprise to Mother and me when he announced that he intended to buy a ship and prove that a sailor could find fulfillment even on the drought-stricken western plains.

I was skeptical. Only the previous summer we had made a journey to Regina, the capital of the province, where I had spent some hours on the banks of Wascana Lake. Wascana was made by men, not God, and by just such men as my father. It boasted two yacht clubs and a fleet of a dozen sailing craft. But it could boast of no water at all. I have never seen anything as pitiful as those little vessels sitting forlornly on the sun-cracked mud of the lake bottom, their seams gaping in the summer heat. I remembered Wascana when Father told us his plans and, supposing that he must remember the phantom lake as well, I asked him if he was contemplating dry-land sailing—on wheels perhaps?

I went to bed early, and without my supper. And I felt a little hurt, for I had only been trying to help.

He bought his ship a few weeks later. She was a sixteen-foot sailing canoe that, by some mischance, had drifted into the arid heart of Saskatchewan. Berthed temporarily in our basement, she looked small and fragile, but she was to prove herself a stout little vessel indeed.

My father spent the balance of the winter laboring over her. With meticulous and loving care he built leeboards, splashboards, a mast, a steering oar, and a set of paddles. He borrowed Mother's sewing machine and made a sail out of the finest Egyptian cotton, shipped to him from Montreal. As for the canoe herself—he burnished her sides with steel wool, scraped them with glass, and painted and repainted until her flanks were as smooth as the surface of a mirror.

Then he applied the final coat of paint—bright green—and with some ceremony christened her *Concepcion*. He *said* that she was so named after an island in the Philippines.

Her launching took place on a day in early May. I helped Father carry her down to the riverbank beside the Twenty-fifth Street bridge and en route we collected an interested group of followers. Vessels of any sort had been unknown in Saskatoon since the time of the prairie schooners, and *Concepcion* was an eye-catching maiden in her own right.

As my father went about the task of stepping the mast and preparing the canoe for her first voyage, the crowd of onlookers increased steadily in numbers. High above our heads the ramparts of the bridge darkened with a frieze of spectators. They were all very quiet and very solemn as Father nodded his head to tell me that he was ready, and then I pushed *Concepcion* into her own element.

It was early spring and the Saskatchewan River was still in flood. My father knew all there was to know about water (so he believed) and it had not occurred to him that there would be much difference between the Bay of Quinte and the South Saskatchewan. There was a good breeze blowing and it riffled the surging brown surface of the water, effectively concealing the telltale swirls and vortexes beneath. The watchers on the bridge, on the other hand, knew a good deal about the nature of prairie rivers in the spring, and there may have been something funereal about the hush that lay upon them as they watched Father and *Concepcion* take to the stream.

The launching took place several hundred feet above the bridge, but by the time Father had everything shipshape, and was able to raise his eyes to look about, the bridge had inexplicably changed its position in relation to him. It was now several hundred yards behind him, and receding at a positively terrifying rate of speed. He became extremely active. He ran up the sail and began hauling in the sheet in an effort to come about.

From the parapets, where I now stood watching with the rest, there came a gasp of mingled awe and admiration. Most of the watchers had never seen a sailing vessel before and they had always understood that sail was an old-fashioned and painfully slow way of getting about. Their eyes were being opened.

Concepcion was acting strangely. She would not come about, for the current was stronger than the breeze. She resolutely skittered downstream, making about twelve knots. She should not have been making five in that light air, and my father knew it. He began to understand about the current. He got out his paddle and with almost demoniac frenzy strove to bring her head upstream. He was successful in the end, but by that time he and *Concepcion* were no more than a rapidly diminishing dot upon the distant surface of the river.

Some of the men standing on the bridge beside me began making bets as to when Father would reach the town of Prince Albert, some hundreds of miles downstream. But it was clear that my father did not really want to reach Prince Albert. He was sailing the canoe now with a grim determination and a skill that he had probably never before been called upon to use. He wanted very badly to come back to Saskatoon.

Concepcion beat back and forth across the river like a wood chip on a frothing millrace. She tacked and beat, and though she kept her head resolutely upstream—and though she was sailing like a witch—she nevertheless kept diminishing in our view until at last she vanished altogether in the bright distance to the north.

One of the men near me glanced at his watch and spoke to his companion. "Eleven o'clock. 'Course, he'll be a mite slower now, goin' backward that

way, but I reckon he'll hit the Prince Albert bridge by suppertime. I'll lay you fifty cents he does."

He would have lost his bet, however, for Father and *Concepcion* did not go to Prince Albert after all. They might have done so had they not been fortunate enough to run aground some ten miles below Saskatoon. Shortly after midnight they arrived home together, in a farm cart that was being towed by two noncommittal horses.

The setback to my father's design was only temporary. "Never mind," he said at breakfast the next day. "Wait till the spring flood passes, and *then* we'll see."

But what we saw when the flood was gone was not encouraging. The South

Saskatchewan was back to normal, and normal consisted of a desert expanse of mud bars with here and there an expiring pool of trapped brown scum and, in a few very favored places, a sluggish trickle of moving water.

It was a sight that would have discouraged any man except my father. He refused to be defeated. He had made his plans, and the river would simply have to conform to them. That was the way he was.

His plans suited me well enough, for we closed up our rented house and moved our old caravan some ten miles south of the city to the Saskatoon Golf and Country Club. Here, on the wooded banks of the Saskatchewan, we established our summer residence.

My time was my own, for the summer holidays had begun, but my father had to commute to work in the city every day. He might easily have done so by car, but he had *planned* to commute by water and he refused to be dissuaded by the uncooperativeness of nature.

At seven o'clock on the first Monday morning he and *Concepcion* set out bravely, and full of confidence in one another. But when they returned late that evening, it was as passengers in, and on, a friend's automobile. My father was very weary; and uncommunicative about the day's adventures. It was not until years later he admitted to me that he had actually walked eight of the ten miles to Saskatoon, towing *Concepcion* behind him through the shallows, or carrying her on his shoulders across sandbars. There had been a brief but exciting interlude with one sandbar that turned out to be quicksand, too, but on this he would not dwell.

Through the next few days he wisely, but reluctantly, commuted in Eardlie, but then there was a rainfall somewhere to the south and the river rose a few inches. Eardlie was again abandoned, and *Concepcion* returned to a place of favor. During the weeks that followed she and Father became intimately familiar with the multitudes of sandbars, the quicksands, and the other mysteries of the shrunken river's channels. And to the astonishment of all observers, my father began to make a success of his water route to the office. It was true that he still walked almost as far as he was able to paddle, but at least he was spared the ignominy of having to haul the canoe along in front of an audience, for a relatively deep channel running through the city enabled him to paddle the final mile of his route to the landing place near the Bessborough Hotel, with Hiawathan dignity.

He would not leave *Concepcion* on the riverbank to await his return, but carried her with him right to the library building. The first few times that he came trotting through the morning traffic in the city center with the green canoe balanced gracefully on his shoulders he caused some comment among the passers-by. But after a week or two people ceased to stare at him and no one, with the exception of a few ultraconservative ice-wagon horses, so much as gave him a second glance. He and *Concepcion* had become an unremarked part of the local scene.

Mutt often accompanied Father and *Concepcion* downriver. He quickly developed the requisite sense of balance and would stand in the bow, his paws on the narrow foredeck, poised like a canine gargoyle. This was not mere posturing on his part either, for he had taken it on himself to give warning when the canoe approached shallow water, or a hidden bar. His efficiency as a pilot was not high, despite his good intentions, for he was notoriously shortsighted. Nor could he, as they say, "read water." After a hysterical outburst prompted by a current boil that he had mistaken for a submerged log, he would very likely be staring placidly into space when *Concepcion* ran hard aground. If the canoe was traveling at any speed Mutt would be catapulted overboard to land on his face in the muddy water. He took such mishaps in good part, and would return to his piloting duties with increased vigilance.

Father was able to paddle *Concepcion* (more or less) on the river, but that mean-natured trickle gave him no opportunity to sail. Since it was sailing he really craved, he was forced to look for other waters, and one weekend he announced that we would visit Manitou Lake—a vast saline slough that lies some hundred miles from Saskatoon.

Manitou is one of the saltiest bodies of water in the world and *Concepcion* was not designed to float in a medium that was hardly more fluid than molasses. She would have no part of Manitou. When we launched her, she hardly wet her keel, but sat on the surface of the lake like a duck upon a slab of ice.

My father was annoyed by her behavior and set about forcing his will upon her by loading her with rocks. It took an unbelievable number of boulders to force her down to her marks, and when Father and I finally clambered aboard, it was to find her about as maneuverable as a concrete coffin floating in gelatin. The water in which she stuck was so thick with salt that I could almost hear the stuff rasping on her sleek sides. And when we hoisted the sail, the wind had as little effect upon her as it would have had upon the Carnegie-built walls of the Saskatoon Public Library itself.

My father was infuriated by *Concepcion*'s lack of response, and unwisely began to jettison the ballast. He had heaved half a dozen large boulders overside when the canoe decided she had had enough. One gunwale rose buoyantly while the other sank, and in short seconds we were floating on a serene sea, while below us *Concepcion* was slowly dragged toward the bottom by her bellyful of stone.

We were in no danger. It was physically impossible for an unweighted human body to sink in Manitou Lake. On the contrary, we rode so high out of the water that we had trouble navigating to the nearby shore. And when we came to salvaging *Concepcion*, who lay in some ten feet of water, the unnatural qualities of Manitou posed a serious problem. We found that we simply could not dive. It was a most eerie experience, for we could not force ourselves more than a foot below the surface. In the end, Father had to weight himself—like a South Sea pearl diver—with a basket full of stones. Clinging to this with one hand, he managed to reach the sunken ship and fasten a line to a thwart. Then he rather thoughtlessly let go of the basket. He came up from the depths like a playful salmon leaping after a fly, shot half out of the water, and fell back with a resounding thwack that must have hurt him almost as much as had *Concepcion*'s behavior.

But, in the end, the frustrations which beset my father's desire to sail again were no match for his perseverance. In August of that memorable year we hitched the caravan to Eardlie, placed *Concepcion* on the roof, and went off on a dogged search for sailing waters. And we found them. Far to the north, in the jack-pine country beyond Prince Albert, we came to a place called Emma Lake, and it was an honest lake, filled with honest water, and caressed by amiable winds.

We launched *Concepcion* with trepidation—for there had been so many unfortunate episodes in the past. Then we climbed aboard, and hoisted sail.

It was the kind of day that graces the western plains, and only them. The sky was crystalline and limitless, and the hard sun cut the surface of the lake into a myriad of brilliant shards. Flocks of black terns swirled in the westerly breeze that came down on us from the pine forests and gently filled *Concepcion*'s sail, bellowing it into a curve as beautiful as any wing. She came alive.

We sailed that day—all of it, until the sun went sickly behind the blue shield of smoke from distant forest fires, and sank away taking the breeze with it. And we sailed aboard a little ship whose swift and delicate motion was more than sufficient reward for the rebuffs that we had suffered.

In the Arctic

[My fifteenth birthday] brought with it the most memorable present I ever received.

My great uncle Frank Farley [had] concluded that I was showing promise as an ornithologist. Without letting me know what he had in mind, he made a proposal to my parents.

Every June for the past five years, Frank had made a journey to the sub-arctic community of Churchill on Hudson Bay. This was a one-time Hudson's Bay Company post which, in 1927, had been selected as the site for an ocean port from which prairie grain could be shipped to Europe. Over the next several years, a railroad was built north across more than five hundred miles of muskeg and spruce forest to service the new port.

Quite incidentally this last great achievement of North American railroading also provided a means for naturalists to reach a unique concentration point on the Arctic flyway of millions of migrating waterfowl and wading birds. Some individuals of many species which flew this route in spring remained on the tundra near Churchill to nest and lay their eggs. The eggs were the magnet which drew my uncle north. He planned to go to Churchill again in June of 1936, and proposed to take me with him as an egg collector.

My parents gave their assent and details were agreed upon by letter. However, Angus and Helen decided to keep me in the dark until my birthday. This was just as well. Had I known earlier what was transpiring, I would have been able to think of nothing else. When at last it was revealed to me, the proposal was as irresistibly entrancing as the prospect of a trip to the moon might be to a youth of today.

Frank was to pick me up on June 5 when his train passed through Saskatoon. Since this would be more than two weeks before school ended, it posed a problem. My parents, bless them, did not mind my missing that much school time but the principal of Nutana Collegiate would have to authorize such a departure from the rules. I do not know if he would have done so on his own. I do know that [my science teacher] represented my interests to such effect that the day after my birthday he was able to bring word that not only would I be permitted to leave school early, I would also be excused from writing the end-of-term examinations. For that intervention, if for nothing else, I owe him a lifelong debt of gratitude.

There remained the problems of assembling my outfit—and of mastering my impatience until June 5 arrived.

Angus had read widely on Arctic subjects so he was the expert on what I should take with me. The outfit he finally assembled would have better suited a member of one of Peary's polar expeditions but my father had so much fun gathering it all together that none of us had the heart to bring him down to earth. Uncle Frank did that in due course. When I eventually embarked, I left behind such items as a patented Scott-of-the-Antarctic-style tent large enough to house eight men; a sleeping bag as bulky as a small hay rick and guaranteed to keep one warm at sixty below zero; a manual on how to train and handle dog teams; and an ingenious set of interlocking cooking pots which weighed about as much as I did. I suspect that my father may have been secretly planning a polar expedition of his own since, so far as I know, none of the rejects was ever returned to the store from which it came.

On June 5, according to Helen's diary, "Bunje up at 3:00 a.m. No peace for any of us until 7:30 when Uncle Frank's train arrived and we went to meet it. Bunje terribly excited."

That I was. When Uncle Frank's rangy great frame swung down from the steps of the parlor car, I could hardly have been more agitated if God himself had alighted.

I had not previously met Frank in the flesh and he certainly seemed bigger than life. He stood a lean six feet three inches tall in knee-length, lace-up boots. His head, under a soft felt hat, was a mountain crag dominated by the famous (in the family) Farley nose. He had the washed-out stare of a turkey vulture. All in all, he was the most intimidating figure of a man I had ever encountered.

Now he was smiling. One ham hand swept down and gripped my shoulder so powerfully I wanted to squeal like a puppy that has been stepped on.

"So this is the bird-boy, eh?" Frank boomed, shaking my seventy-five-pound frame none too gently. "Not much bigger than a bird at that."

He let me go and turned to introduce a slight, dark-haired young man who had descended behind him—Albert Wilks, a twenty-year-old schoolteacher who had also been signed on as an egg collector.

Tipped off by Angus who was always *au fait* with the press, a reporter from the *Star Phoenix* was on hand to interview the "world-famous ornithologist." The interview was conducted over breakfast in Wang's Chinese Café where, for the first time, I heard what Frank had in mind.

We would camp on the tundra near Churchill, he told us, until the pack ice covering the inland sea called Hudson Bay slackened enough to let us travel in seagoing canoes accompanied by two Barrenground trappers, "Eskimo" Harris and "Windy" Smith, north up the coast to the Seal River. We would then set up a base camp and spend a month on and around the Seal, making the first scientific collection of animal life from the region. It was to be hoped, Frank added portentously, that the collection would not only encompass birds' eggs but would also include white wolves, Arctic foxes, and seals.

My breakfast went untouched. I was so bedazzled by visions of what lay ahead that I may have been slightly catatonic by the time my parents saw the three of us aboard the noon train. My mother thought I looked angelic, but stunned would probably have been closer to the truth.

By dinner time the train had left the "big prairie" behind and was running north and east through poplar and birch parkland. At midnight it came to a halt beside a cluster of shacks and a small station which bore the tantalizing name "Hudson Bay Junction." Here we disembarked with all our gear to await the arrival of a train from Winnipeg which would take us on to The Pas.

At 3:30 a.m. a baleful whistle roused me from broken sleep on a station bench. We stumbled aboard and found ourselves in the nineteenth century. Our chariot to the North was a colonist car built in the 1880s to ferry European immigrants westward from Montreal after they had been disgorged from the bowels of trans-Atlantic sailing ships.

Colonist cars were designed to transport the impoverished at minimum cost. No effort had been spared to preclude anything smacking of comfort. The seats were made of hardwood slats. They faced each other in pairs and could be slid together in such a way that each pair formed a crowded sleeping platform for four people. There was no upholstery of any kind, no mattresses, and no cushions. Lighting was provided by oil lamps whose chimneys were dark with age and soot. Our car was heated by a coal stove upon which passengers could boil water for tea and for washing, and do their cooking. Some colonist cars had flush toilets of a sort but not ours. There was only a hole in the floor of the toilet cubicle through which one could watch the ties flicker past—an exercise that gave me vertigo.

The car was only half full when we boarded so we were able to claim a two-seat "section" for ourselves. We were lucky. At The Pas—the last settlement en route to the Arctic—the car would become so crowded that some people would have to lay their bed rolls in the aisles.

Our fellow passengers were mostly trappers of European, Indian, and mixed blood, accompanied by their women and children. We also had two Roman Catholic missionaries, and the engineer and three crew members of a Hudson's Bay Company schooner which had spent the winter frozen in the ice at Churchill. All these were exotic enough, but most fascinating was a trio of Eskimos on the first lap of a long voyage back to their homes in the high Arctic after having spent many months in a tuberculosis sanitorium in southern Manitoba. They spoke no English and, since nobody else in the car spoke Inuktitut, I could not begin to satisfy my enormous curiosity about them.

We reached The Pas at noon. Despite its curious name, it was no more than a ramshackle little frontier village serving as the southern terminus of the Hudson Bay Railway which, all in its own good time, would carry us to Churchill. The northern train was made up of a long string of wheat-filled boxcars to which our colonial car, a baggage car, and a caboose were appended like the tail of a dog.

At dusk we pulled out of The Pas and began the long haul northward at a sedate twenty miles an hour—a speed we were never to exceed and which we often fell far below.

By now we had entered the true boreal forest and were bumping along through a seemingly endless black spruce shroud, broken here and there by quagmires and little ponds. Frank joined me at one of the dirt-streaked windows as I looked out upon a broad sweep of saturated "moose pasture" thinly dotted with tamarack trees.

"That's muskeg, my boy. You'll see enough of it before we're through. Fact, most of what you'll see from now on until we reach the edge of the Barrens is just like this. That's why the train is called the Muskeg Express. By some. Some call it the Muskeg Crawler and claim you could walk the five hundred miles from The Pas to Churchill quicker."

Our home on wheels now began to come vigorously to life. Someone stoked up the stove with billets of birch and soon the aroma of bannocks frying in pork fat assailed us, mixed with the molasses-laden reek of the "twist" tobacco most trappers smoked.

Blackened tea billies came to the boil and were passed along from seat to seat so that everyone could fill his or her mug with a smoky brew heavily laced with sugar. Bert heated us up a pan of pork and beans. A Cree woman across the aisle suckled a young baby at her breast while feeding an older one canned milk out of a beer bottle...and I stared until my eyes bulged.

This being the first night out of The Pas, there was a considerable celebration. Lusty songs were sung in Cree, French, English, and unidentifiable tongues.

Bottles were freely passed around. Some of the men began playing cards and there was a brief fight during which I thought I saw the flash of a knife. The noise level mounted by the minute.

At this juncture one of the train men (there was no conductor) came along and leaned down to yell something in Frank's ear. My uncle nodded and pulled me to my feet. "Get your bed roll!" he bellowed.

We swayed to the end of our car, passed through the baggage car (which contained several canoes and a line of Indian dogs chained to a cable along one wall), then we were in the caboose.

"You'll sleep here," Frank told me. "It'll keep you out of trouble. And it'll be a damn sight quieter."

So it was, but much duller. Although I had a bunk and mattress to myself, I regretted missing what might be happening in the colonist car.

During the morning of the second day out of The Pas, we crossed the mighty Nelson River flowing eastward into Hudson Bay. The right-of-way now pointed due north and the train ran—crawled, rather—on a road-bed that literally floated on muskeg. The muskeg in turn floated on permafrost—the eternally frozen underpinnings of a land which, even in the first week of June, was still crosshatched by huge snowdrifts and whose lakes and major rivers were still frozen. According to Uncle Frank, spring was very late this year and he grew gloomy about the prospects for traveling on Hudson Bay.

The uncertain footing now slowed the Muskeg Express to something less than a crawl and there was little to see of interest in the snow-striped land-scape. I tried entertaining myself by clocking the slow passage of the black and white mile boards nailed to telegraph poles. By Mile 380 I had tired of this game and was reduced to reading a book. It appeared that nothing was going to happen until we finally reached Churchill.

But at Mile 410 something *did* happen. I had earlier noticed that the succession of stunted spruce trees was being pierced by openings running out of the north-west. When I asked Uncle Frank about these, he explained that they were fingers of tundra thrusting southward from the vast Arctic plains which comprise the Barrenlands.

I went back to the cupola with renewed interest and had just seen Mile

410 slide slowly past when the rusty whistle of the old engine began to give tongue with a reckless disregard for steam pressure. At the first blast I looked forward over the humped backs of the grain cars.

A flowing, brown river was surging out of the shrunken forest to the eastward, plunging through the drifts to pour across the track ahead of us. But this was no river of water—it was a river of life. I had my field glasses to my eyes in an instant and the stream dissolved into its myriad parts. Each was a long-legged caribou.

"C'est la Foule!" The French-Canadian brakeman had climbed up into the cupola beside me. It is the Throng! This was the name given by early French explorers to the most spectacular display of animal life still to be seen on our continent or perhaps anywhere on earth—the mass migration of the Barrenland caribou, the wild reindeer of the Canadian North.

The train whistle continued to blow with increasing exasperation but the oncoming hordes did not deviate from their own right-of-way, which clearly took precedence over ours. They did not hurry their steady, loose-limbed lope. At last the engineer gave up his attempts to intimidate this oblivious multitude. With a resigned whiffle of steam the train came to a halt.

For an hour that river of caribou flowed unhurriedly into the north-west. Then it began to thin and soon was gone. The old engine gathered its strength; passengers who had alighted to stretch their legs climbed back aboard and we, too, continued north.

The dwarf trees began to march along beside us again but I did not see them. I was intoxicated by the vision of the Throng. Many years later it would inexorably draw me back to the domain of the caribou.

The morning after our arrival [in Churchill] we loaded our gear on a hand jigger—a little rail car propelled by manpower. With Uncle Frank and Bert pumping the handles we rattled out of Churchill on a narrow-gauge spur line. Our destination was an abandoned construction shack standing in lonely decrepitude on the bald tundra some eight miles south-east of Churchill. Shanty-roofed, with tar-paper walls, it contained a rusty barrel stove, two double-tiered bunks, a broken table, and not much else except the frozen corpse of a white Arctic fox that had apparently jumped in through a broken window and failed to find its way out again.

We settled in to await the withdrawal of the pack ice from the coast of Hudson Bay. As it happened, the ice never did withdraw while we remained in Churchill, so we stayed on at the Black Shack, as Bert named it, for the duration.

"At" but seldom "in." Uncle Frank would have made (and maybe was in a previous incarnation) an effective slave driver. Since the nights never got wholly dark, he regarded sleeping as a waste of time.

"Look about you," he lectured me as I tried to lie abed one shivering morning when our water pails had an inch of ice on them. "The birds out on the tundra haven't slept a wink. Too much to do! Too busy! And here it is 4:00 a.m. and you want more sleep! Up and at 'em, sonny!"

Bert was our cook. Burned cornmeal porridge was his specialty but we also ate canned beans; bannock spread with molasses; fat bacon and, on special occasions, cornmeal mush that had been allowed to solidify overnight before being sliced and fried in bacon fat. Frank explained that he had intended us to "live off the land" at Seal River: "Lots of seal meat; maybe a haunch or two of caribou." But since there were neither seals nor caribou where we were, Frank spent much of his time roaming the surrounding tundra blasting ducks and ptarmigan with his double-barreled shotgun. Bert made watery concoctions that he called Mulligan stew from some of these victims of my uncle's gun, but the corpses of many ended up in a nearby ditch which served as our garbage dump.

I agonized a little about this apparently wanton killing of breeding birds at the peak of the nesting season until Uncle Frank put me straight.

"Don't be soft, boy. There's millions more out there. We're doing this for science. I measure every specimen I shoot and note the condition of its plumage. Science needs to know these things."

Years would pass before I would realize that collecting expeditions such as ours were little more than high-grade plundering operations conducted in the hallowed name of Science. However, for the moment my qualms were stilled and I could go about my duties with an easy conscience.

My duties were straightforward enough.

"Find every nest you can," Frank instructed Bert and me. "The rarer the bird the better. If the nest hasn't got a full clutch, mark the spot and leave it 'til it has. If you aren't sure what species it is, shoot the parent bird and bring it back when you bring the eggs."

With half a dozen tobacco cans filled with cotton wool in our haversacks together with our lunches, Bert and I would be out every day and all day, unless it was pouring rain or, as happened sometimes, snowing so hard that searching for nests would have been useless. I was a good nest finder and I loved the work. When I flushed a rarity, such as a Hudsonian Godwit, and found four eggs ready for the taking, I would feel as elated as if I had found four gold nuggets.

So many waterfowl and wading birds clustered on the tundra that there seemed hardly room enough for all of them to nest. As I sloshed across the still-half-frozen morass of water and mossy tussocks, curlews, several species of plovers, many varieties of sandpipers, and numerous kinds of ducks would rise before me, filling the air with their cries of alarm.

I took a heavy toll from their nests.

Having made my way back to the shack for supper, dog-tired and, like as not, soaking wet from falling through the rotting ice of a pond, I would spread my day's "take" on the table to be admired. Once I unpacked thirteen clutches from my tobacco cans, bettering anything Bert or Frank himself had so far collected in a single day. Frank rewarded me with kind words: "You'll make a good scientist, my boy."

According to my uncle, one egg by itself had no scientific value so we always took the full clutch, thereby ensuring that, because the season was too short to allow the birds to nest again, the adult pair would raise no young that year. The real truth of the matter was that the eggs had no *commercial* value unless a whole clutch could be displayed as a unit in a collector's glass-topped case. This was something else I was still to learn.

Lemmings were all around us, both inside and outside the shack. It was a peak year in their seven-year cycle of abundance and they were making the most of it. Friendly little creatures looking not unlike small hamsters, they would sometimes crawl across my lap as I sat on a tussock eating my lunch. They would also run all over the cabin floor, paying no heed to us until Bert lost patience and tried to sweep them out the door.

Egg collecting was not all beer and skittles. One morning the sun shone, the snow was melting, and it really felt like spring so the three of us set off together to explore the wall of granite which fringed the still-frozen bay like a titanic dyke. We were after the eggs of rough-legged hawks (famed lemming hunters) who occupied a chain of nests built at half-mile intervals on ledges along the seaward face of the dyke.

According to my uncle these nests were ancestral possessions used by generations of rough-legs. Not all were occupied every year. The year after the lemming population "crashed," at the bottom of its cycle, the hawks might use only every second or third nest and, instead of laying a clutch of four or five eggs, might lay only one or two. They were able to adjust their reproductive capacity to the available food supply, something human beings seem incapable of doing.

Because 1936 was a good lemming year every nest held a full clutch. Bert and I had to gather these by scaling the face of the wall or by descending from above. Either way it was a risky business. We had each delivered two clutches to Frank waiting below on the ice-cluttered beach when the hawks decided things had gone far enough.

The ones we had already robbed had been following us, shrieking their distress as they soared overhead. Now, as I began to ascend to my third nest, they began to descend. One by one, like a squadron of attacking fighter aircraft, they stooped on me, talons outstretched and beaks gaping wide. The first one missed by no more than a foot and made me cower against the cliff wall. The second struck home.

My head was buffeted hard against the rock by fiercely beating wings. I raised an arm to protect myself and it was raked from wrist to elbow by sharp talons. For a horrible instant I thought I was going to fall; then Frank's shotgun bellowed and my attacker spun away, still screaming defiance.

I did not wait for the next attack but slid down the face of the cliff to land, scared and shaking, on the beach. Bert bound up my arm with his handkerchief but my uncle offered scant sympathy. He was eyeing the circling hawks and the nest which still contained the eggs he coveted.

"You must have done something to upset them," he said crossly, which surely had to be the understatement of the year.

Summer exploded during the last week of June. Overnight the temperature soared into the sixties and, but for the hordes of mosquitoes emerging from the tundra ponds, we could have gone around naked. The remaining ice and snow shrank visibly before our eyes. The egg-laying season was coming to an end and soon it would be time for us to leave.

There were some chores to be attended to first. Foremost of these, as far as I was concerned, was collecting one more set of rough-legged hawk's eggs to compensate for the clutch I had failed to get. Frank had said nothing directly to me about this but I knew it was on his mind.

One warm and sunny morning I set off to the coastal ridge. I did not go back to the stretch we had already robbed but headed farther east. Nests proved few and far between in this area and it was not until afternoon that I found one, in a cleft of rock fifty feet above the beach. This time I climbed down to it from above, keeping a wary eye on the parent birds wheeling disconsolately overhead. They did not attack and I stole their eggs, wrapped them in cotton wool and packed them in my haversack. That done, I looked about from my high vantage point.

Below me the waters sucked and seethed at stranded ice floes along the shore. Open-water leads criss-crossed the decaying pack to seaward. I looked eastward along the beach and saw a large reddish object. Through my field glasses it revealed itself as the shattered remnant of a ship.

Few things will fire a boy's curiosity as hotly as a wreck, and I hurried off to examine this one. It consisted of the forward half of a small coastal freighter which must have driven ashore many years earlier. I climbed through a maze of twisted, rusty plates until I was standing high on the angled rise of the bow.

And then discovered I was not alone!

Not more than a hundred yards away, three ivory-white bears were ambling unconcernedly towards me. The leader of the trio seemed unbelievably huge, though its followers were not much bigger than a pair of spaniels. I did not need to be a naturalist to know that this was a female polar bear and her cubs.

I was terrified. "Always stay clear of a sow bear with cubs" was a maxim of which I was well aware though, in my case, it had referred to the relatively small black bears of more southern climes. I felt that the warning must apply in spades to the monstrous apparition now padding in my direction with such fluid grace.

I thought of fleeing but to move would have meant revealing myself—and I had no stomach for a race with her! The light breeze was in my favor, blowing towards me, so I could hope the bears might pass by without ever realizing I was crouching in abject fear ten feet above them.

They were within a dozen yards when, for no apparent reason, the female abruptly stopped and reared back on her ample haunches while extending her forelegs for balance. Her immense paws hung down before her, revealing their long, curved claws. Perhaps I moved, or maybe she heard my heart pounding. She looked up and our glances locked. Her black nose wrinkled. She sniffed explosively then, with an astonishing lithesomeness for so huge a beast, slewed around and was off at a gallop in the direction from which she had come, her pups bounding along behind her.

My own departure was almost as precipitate. I fled so fast that the eggs in my pack had become the ingredients for another omelette before I reached Black Shack.

A week later we again boarded the Muskeg Express. The first of a long series of visits I would eventually make to Churchill and on into the mighty sweep of tundra stretching northward from that Arctic gateway was at an end.

On the Salt Seas

Mowat and his friend Jack McClelland dreamed of buying a boat "in which to roam the salt seas over." Mowat went to Newfoundland, where he bought a decidedly unseaworthy vessel. After many misadventures, Mowat and McClelland were ready for their first test of Happy Adventure.

Seamen refer to the first tentative voyage of a newly commissioned ship as her trials. *Happy Adventure*'s trials began at 1400 hours the next day, and so did ours.

It was a "civil" day (in Newfoundland this means the wind is not blowing a full hurricane) and a stiff easterly was whitening the waters of the harbor.

Because this was our first departure, and because we were being watched by most of the inhabitants of Muddy Hole, we felt compelled to leave the stage under full sail.

We did not do too badly. With main, foresail, jib, and jumbo hoisted, Jack cast off our moorings. We sheeted everything home, the heavy sails began to draw, and *Happy Adventure* slowly picked up way. In a few moments she was standing swiftly across the harbor.

In order to get out of the long, narrow harbor of Muddy Hole against an east wind, a vessel under sail must beat to weather—that is, she must tack back and forth against the wind. We were, of course, aware of this necessity. We were also aware that, as we left the stage, directly ahead of us there lay a covey of two dozen dories and skiffs, moored fifty yards offshore. As we approached them I prepared to come about on the other tack.

"Ready about!" I sang out to Jack. Then, pushing the big tiller over, "Hard a'lee!"

Happy Adventure's head came up into the wind. She shook herself a bit, considered whether she would come about or not—and decided not. Her head fell off again and she resumed her original course.

Jack was later to claim that this was one of the few honest things she ever did. He claimed she knew perfectly well what would happen if we ever took her to sea, and so she decided it would be better for all of us if she committed suicide immediately by skewing herself on the rocky shores of her home port, where her bones could rest in peace forever.

I disagree. I think that, never having been under sail before, the poor little vessel simply did not know what was expected of her. I think she was as terrified as I was as she bore down on the defenseless mess of little boats and the rocks that lay beyond them.

It was Jack who saved us all. He did not even pause to curse, but leaped into the engine room with such alacrity that he caught the bullgine sleeping. Before it knew he was there he had spun the flywheel and, even without a prime, the green beast was so surprised she fired. She had been taken totally off guard, but even as she belched into life she struck back at us, thinking to make us pay for our trickery by starting in reverse.

There were a good many people watching from the fish-plant wharf. Since they could not hear the roar of the bullgine above the thunder of the plant machinery they were incredulous of what they saw. Under full sail and snoring bravely along, *Happy Adventure* slowly came to a stop. Then with all sails still set and drawing—she began to back up. The fish plant manager, a worldly man who had several times seen motion picture films, said it was like watching a movie that had been reversed. He said he expected to see the schooner back right up Obie's stage, lower her sails, and go to sleep again.

I would have been happy to have had this happen. To tell the truth I was so unnerved that it was on the tip of my tongue to turn command over to Jack, jump into our little dory which we were towing astern, and abandon the sea forever. However, pride is a terrible taskmaster and I dared not give in to my sounder instincts.

It was now obvious to Jack and to me that we were not going to be able to beat out of the harbor and that we would have to go out under power if we were to get out at all. But neither of us cared to try to make the bullgine change direction and drive the boat ahead. We knew perfectly well she would stop, and refuse to start, and leave us to drift ignominiously ashore. Consequently, *Happy Adventure backed* all the way out of Muddy Hole harbor under full sail. I think it must have been the most reluctant departure in the history of men and ships.

Once we were at sea, and safely clear of the great headlands guarding the harbor mouth, Jack did try to reverse the engine and she reacted as we had known she would. She stopped and would not start. It no longer mattered. *Happy Adventure* lay over on her bilge, took the wind over her port bow, and went bowling off down the towering coast as if she were on her way to a racing rendezvous.

During the next few hours all the miseries, doubts, and distresses of the past weeks vanished from our minds. The little ship sailed like a good witch. She still refused to come about, but this was no great problem in open water since we could jibe her around, and her masts and rigging were so stout that this sometimes dangerous practice threatened her not at all. We sailed her on a broad reach; we sailed her hard on the wind; we let her run, hung-out, with foresail to starboard and mainsail to port; and we had no fault to find with her sea-keeping qualities.

She had, however, some other frailties. The unaccustomed motion of bucketing through big seas under a press of canvas squeezed out most of the fish gunk with which she had sealed her seams, and she began to leak so excessively that Jack had to spend most of his time at the pump. Also, the massive compass I had brought with me from Ontario demonstrated an incredible disdain for convention and insisted on pointing as much as forty degrees off what should have been the correct course. It was apparent that, until we found someone who could adjust the compass, our navigation would have to be, in the time-honored phrase, "by guess and by God." Neither of us was a very good guesser and we did not know how much we could rely on God.

In our temporarily euphoric mood we dared to sail several miles off shore to reconnoiter a belated iceberg. We were circling it at a discreet distance, for the great bergs become unstable in late summer and sometimes turn turtle, setting up tidal waves that can swamp a small vessel, when the sun began to haze over. The Grand Banks fog was rolling in upon the back of the east wind.

We fled before it and *Happy Adventure* carried us swiftly between the headlands of the harbor just as the fog overtook us, providing a gray escort as we ran down the reach and rounded-to in fine style at Obie's stage.

Despite her unorthodox departure, and despite the leaks and the compass, we felt reasonably content with our little vessel and not a little proud of ourselves as well. We were as ready as we would ever be to begin our voyage.

One small difficulty still remained. We had no charts of the east coast of Newfoundland. The lack of charts, combined with a misleading compass and the dead certainty of running into fog, suggested we would do well to ship a pilot until we could make a port where charts could be bought and the compass adjusted.

The obvious choice for a pilot was Enos.* Like most Newfoundland seamen he possessed, we presumed, special senses which are lost to modern man.

---

* Enarchos Coffin, who had built the boat.

He had sailed these waters all his life, often without a compass and usually without charts. When you asked him how he managed to find his way to some distant place he would look baffled and reply:

"Well, me son, I *knows* where it's at."

We needed somebody like that. However, when we broached the matter to Enos he showed no enthusiasm. For a man who was usually as garrulous as an entire pack of politicians, his response was spectacularly succinct.

"No!" he grunted, and for emphasis spat a gob of tobacco juice on our newly painted cabin top.

There was no swaying him either. Persuasion (and Jack is a persuader *par excellence*) got us nowhere. He kept on saying "No" and spitting until the cabin top developed a slippery brown sheen over most of its surface and we were prepared to give up. I was, at any rate, but Jack was made of sterner stuff.

"If the old bustard won't come willingly," Jack told me after Enos left, "we'll shanghai him."

"The hell with him, Jack. Forget it. We'll manage on our own."

"Forget him nothing! If this goddamn boat sinks I'm at least going to have the satisfaction of seeing him sink with it!"

There was no arguing with Jack in a mood like that.

He arranged a small farewell party on board that night. It was one of the gloomiest parties I have ever attended. Six or seven of our fishermen friends squeezed into the cabin and ruminated at lugubrious length on the manifold perils of the sea. When they got tired of that, they began recalling the small schooners that had sailed out of Southern Shore ports and never been heard of again. The list went on and on until even Enos began to grow restive.

"Well, byes," he interjected, "them was mostly poor-built boats. Not fitten to go to sea. Not proper fer it, ye might say. Now you takes a boat like this 'un. Proper built and found. *She* won't be making ary widows on the shore."

This was the opening Jack had been waiting for.

"You're so right, Enos. In a boat as good as this a fellow could sail to hell and back."

Enos eyed Jack with sudden suspicion. "Aye," he replied cautiously. "She be good fer it!"

"*You* certainly wouldn't be afraid to sail in her, now would you, Enos?"
The trap was sprung.

"Well, now, me darlin' man, I don't say as I wouldn't, but a'course…"

"Good enough!" Jack shouted. "Farley, hand me the log. Enos, we'll sign you on as sailing master for the maiden voyage of the finest ship you ever built."

Enos struggled mightily but to no avail. He was under the eyes of six of his peers and one of them, without realizing it, became our ally:

"Sign on, sign on, Enos, me son. We knows you'm not afeard!"

So Enos signed his mark.

Happy Adventure sailed an hour after dawn. It was a fine morning, clear and warm, with a good draft of wind out of the nor'west to help us on our way and to keep the fog off shore. We had intended to sail *at* dawn but Enos did not turn up and when we went to look for him his daughters said he had gone off to haul a herring net. We recognized this as a ruse, and so we searched for him in the most likely place. He was savagely disgruntled when we found him, complaining bitterly that a man couldn't even "do his nature" without being followed. Little by little we coaxed him down to the stage, got him aboard and down below, and before he could rally, we cast off the lines.

Happy Adventure made a brave sight as she rolled down the reach toward the waiting sea. With all sails set and drawing she lay over a little and snored sweetly through the water, actually overtaking and passing two or three belated trap skiffs bound out to the fishing grounds. Their crews grinned cheerfully at us, which is as close to a farewell as a Newfoundland seaman will allow himself. There is bad luck in farewells.

Before we cleared the headlands I celebrated a small ritual that I learned from my father. I poured four stiff glasses of rum. I gave one of these to Enos and one to Jack, and I kept one for myself. The fourth I poured overboard. The Old Man of the Sea is a sailor and he likes his drop of grog. And it is a good thing to be on friendly terms with the Old Man when you venture out upon the gray waters that are his domain.

All that morning we sailed south on a long reach, keeping a two- or three-mile offing from the grim sea cliffs. We came abeam of Cape Ballard and left it behind, then the wind began to fall light and fickle, ghosting for a change. The change came and the wind picked up from sou'east, a dead muzzler right on our bows, bringing the fog in toward us.

Enos began to grow agitated. We were approaching Cape Race, the southeast "corner" of Newfoundland and one of the most feared places in the western ocean. Its peculiar menace lies in the tidal currents that sweep past it. They are totally unpredictable. They can carry an unwary vessel, or one blinded by fog, miles off her true course and so to destruction on the brooding rocks ashore.

In our innocence Jack and I were not much worried, and when Enos insisted that we down sail and start the engine we were inclined to mock him. He did not like this and withdrew into sullen taciturnity, made worse by the fact that I had closed off the rum rations while we were at sea. Finally, to please him, we started the bullgine, or rather Jack did, after a blasphemous half hour's struggle.

The joys of the day were now all behind us. Somber clouds began closing off the sky; the air grew chill, presaging the coming of the fog; and the thunderous blatting of the unmuffled bullgine deafened us, while the slow strokes of the great piston shook the little boat as an otter shakes a trout.

By four o'clock we still had reasonably good visibility and were abeam of Cape Race—and there we stuck. The engine thundered and the water boiled under our counter, but we got no farther on our way. Hour after hour the massive highlands behind the cape refused to slip astern. Jack and I finally began to comprehend something of the power of the currents. Although we were making five knots through the water a lee bow tide was running at almost the same speed against us.

The fog was slow in coming but the wall of gray slid inexorably nearer. At six-thirty Jack went below to rustle up some food. An instant later his head appeared in the companionway. The air of casual insouciance, which was as much a part of his seagoing gear as his jaunty yachting cap, had vanished.

"Christ!" he cried, and it was perhaps partly a prayer. "This bloody boat is sinking!"

I jumped to join him and found that he was undeniably right. Water was already sluicing across the floor boards in the main cabin. Spread-eagling the engine for better purchase, Jack began working the handle of the pump as if his life depended on it. It dawned on me his life *did* depend on it, and so did mine.

The next thing I knew Enos had shouldered me aside. Taking one horrified look at the private swimming pool inside *Happy Adventure*, he shrieked:

"Lard Jasus, byes, she's gone!"

It was hardly the remark we needed to restore our faith in him or in his boat. Still yelling, he went on to diagnose the trouble.

He told us the stuffing box had fallen off. This meant that the ocean was free to enter the boat through the large hole in the sternpost that housed the vessel's shaft. And since we could not reach it there was nothing we could do about it.

Enos now retreated into a mental room of his own, a dark hole filled with fatalistic thoughts. However, by giving him a bottle of rum to cherish, I managed to persuade him to take the tiller (the little boat had meanwhile been going in circles) and steer a course for Trepassey Bay, fifteen miles to the eastward, where I thought we might just manage to beach the vessel before she sank.

There was never any question of abandoning her. Our dory, so-called, was a little plywood box barely capable of carrying one man. Life-preservers would have been useless, because we were in the Labrador Current where the waters are so cold that a man cannot survive immersion in them for more than a few minutes.

By dint of furious pumping, Jack and I found we could almost hold the water level where it was, although we could not gain upon the inflow. And so we pumped. The engine thundered on. We pumped. The minutes stretched into hours and we pumped. The fog held off, which was one minor blessing, and we pumped. The engine roared and the heat became so intense that we were sweating almost as much water back into the bilges as we were pumping out. We pumped. The tidal current slackened and turned and began to help us on our way. We pumped.

Occasionally one of us crawled on deck to breathe and to rest his agonized muscles for a moment. At eight o'clock I stuck my head out of the companionway and saw the massive headland of Mistaken Point a mile or so to leeward. I glanced at Enos. He was staring straight ahead, his eyes half shut and his mouth pursed into a dark pit of despair. He had taken out his dentures, a thing he always did in moments of stress. When I called out to tell him we were nearly holding the leak he gave no sign of hearing but continued staring over the bow as if he beheld some bleak and terrible vision from which he could not take his attention for a moment. Not at all cheered I ducked back into the engine room.

And then the main pump jammed.

That pump was a fool of a thing that had no right to be aboard a boat. Its innards were a complicated mass of springs and valves that could not possibly digest the bits of flotsam, jetsam, and codfish floating in the vessel's bilge. But, fool of a thing or not, it was our only hope.

It was dark by this time, so Jack held a flashlight while I unbolted the pump's face plate. The thing contained ten small coil springs and all of them leaped for freedom the instant the plate came off. They ricocheted off the cabin sides like a swarm of manic bees and fell, to sink below the surface of the water in the bilges.

It does not seem possible, but we found them all. It took twenty-five or thirty minutes of groping with numbed arms under oily, icy water, but we found them all, re-installed them, put back the face plate, and again began to pump.

Meanwhile, the water had gained four inches. It was now over the lower part of the flywheel and less than two inches below the top of the carburetor. The flywheel spun a niagara of spray onto the red-hot exhaust pipe, turning the dark and roaring engine room into a sauna bath. We pumped.

Jack crawled on deck for a breather and immediately gave a frantic yell. For a second I hesitated. I did not think I had the fortitude to face a new calamity—but a second urgent summons brought me out on deck. Enos was frozen at the helm and by the last light of day I could see he was steering straight toward a wall of rock which loomed above us, no more than three hundred yards away.

I leaped for the tiller. Enos did not struggle but meekly moved aside. His expression had changed and had become almost beatific. It may have been the rum that did it—Enos was at peace with himself and with the Fates.

"We'd best run her onto the rocks," he explained mildly, "than be drowned in the cold, cold water."

Jack went back to the pump, and I put the vessel on a course to skirt the threatening cliffs. We were not impossibly far from Trepassey Bay, and there still seemed to be a chance we could reach the harbor and beach the vessel on a non-lethal shore.

At about eleven o'clock I saw a flashing light ahead and steered for it. When I prodded him, Enos confirmed that it might be the buoy marking the entrance to Trepassey harbor. However, before we reached it the fog overtook us and the darkness became total. We felt our way past the light-buoy and across the surrounding shoals with only luck and the Old Man to guide us.

As we entered the black gut which we hoped was the harbor entrance, I did not need Jack's warning shout to tell me that our time had about run out. The bullgine had begun to cough and splutter. The water level had reached her carburetor and, tough as she was, she could not remain alive for long on a mixture of gasoline and salt sea water.

Within Trepassey harbor all was inky black. No lights could be seen on the invisible shore. I steered blindly ahead, knowing that sooner or later we must strike the land. Then the engine coughed, stopped, picked up again, coughed, and stopped for good. Silently, in that black night, the little ship ghosted forward.

Jack came tumbling out on deck for there was no point in remaining below while the vessel floundered. He had, and I remember this with great clarity, a flashlight in his mouth and a bottle of rum in each hand...

...At that moment *Happy Adventure*'s forefoot hit something. She jarred a little, made a strange sucking sound, and the motion went out of her.

"I t'inks," said Enos as he nimbly relieved Jack of one of the bottles, "I t'inks we's runned ashore!"

Jack believes *Happy Adventure* has a special kind of homing instinct. He may be right. Certainly she is never happier than when she is lying snuggled up

against a working fish-plant. Perhaps she identifies fish plants with the natal womb, which is not so strange when one remembers she was built in a fish-plant yard and that she spent the many months of her refit as a semi-permanent fixture in the fish-plant slip at Muddy Hole.

In any event when she limped into Trepassey she unerringly found her way straight to her spiritual home. Even before we began playing flashlights on our surroundings we knew this was so. The old familiar stench rose all around us like a dank miasma.

The flashlights revealed that we had run ashore on a gently shelving beach immediately alongside a massively constructed wharf. Further investigation had to be delayed because the tide was falling and the schooner was in danger of keeling over on her bilge. Jack made a jump and managed to scale the face of the wharf. He caught the lines I threw him and we rigged a spider web of ropes from our two masts to the wharf timbers to hold the vessel upright when all the water had drained away from under her.

When she seemed secure I joined Jack on the dock and cautiously we went exploring. The fog was so thick that our lights were nearly useless, and we practically bumped into the first human being we encountered. He was the night watchman for Industrial Seafood Packers, a huge concern to whose dock we were moored. After we had convinced the watchman that we did not have a cargo of fish to unload, but were only mariners in distress, he came aboard.

He seemed genuinely incredulous to find we did not have a radar set. How, he asked, had we found our way into the harbor? How had we missed striking the several draggers anchored in the fairway? And how, in hell's own name (his words), had we found the plant and managed to come alongside the wharf without hitting the L-shaped end where the cod-oil factory stood in lonely grandeur?

Since we could not answer these questions we evaded them, leaving him with the suspicion, which spread rapidly around Trepassey, that we were possessed by an occult power. Witches and warlocks have not yet vanished from the outport scene in Newfoundland.

The watchman was a generous man and he told us we could stay at the wharf as long as we wished. He felt, however, that we might be happier if we moored a hundred feet farther to seaward.

"'Tis the poipe, ye know; the poipe what carries off the gurry from the plant. Ye've moored hard alongside o' she."

Happy Adventure had come home with a vengeance and, for all I know, it may have *been* vengeance at that.

Becoming a Writer

The Young Naturalist

During the autumn of 1934 I had begun to acquire a bit of a reputation at school as an interesting eccentric. Although many of my contemporaries (mostly in the hockey and baseball crowd) continued to deride me as a "sissy nature kid," others were impressed by the remarkable relationship which existed between me and Mutt, one which seemed to verge on the paranormal. It was claimed by some (and who was I to deny it?) that I could communicate with beasts by means of mental telepathy, something which was all the rage in those times. My possession of a witch doctor's bundle composed of dried tarantulas and poisonous centipedes (a present from my uncle Jack who had picked it up in Africa during the war) did my reputation no harm, and the fact that I was known to share my bedroom with bats was thought fascinating by some, if in a repulsive sort of way. These things produced a sufficient measure of regard from a small group of other youngsters to enable me to create the Beaver Club of Amateur Naturalists.

Initially the club consisted of four boys and three girls, one of the latter being Tom McPherson's daughter, Kathleen. All candidates for membership (excepting Kathleen, with whom I was enamored and who therefore had dispensation) were required to submit to a rigorous initiation. Each had to be able to list from memory one hundred birds, twenty-five mammals, and fifty fish, reptiles, or insects. Each had to undertake at least one ten-mile nature hike a month. Each had to write, then read aloud at one of our regular weekly meetings, a four-page essay about nature. Finally, each had to donate a natural object of some considerable value to the Saskatchewan National Animal Museum.

I had actually begun the museum some time before founding the club and shortly after my first exploration of the professor's house.* In the basement I

---

* The Mowats were living in Saskatoon in the house of a professor who had rented them his home while he was away on sabbatical.

had found a large, wood-paneled room whose walls were lined, floor to ceiling, with glass-fronted book shelves. Recognizing their potential as display cases for my ever-growing collection of bits and pieces of animate creation, I staked my claim on the room (which had been the professor's study) as a place in which to do my homework. Since neither Angus nor Helen had any other use in mind for it, they let me have it.

One of the first things the Beaver Club did was to devote a Saturday afternoon, when my parents were absent from home, to pulling the professor's hundreds of academic tomes off their shelves and hauling them out to the garage. We stacked them between the lawn mower and the lawn roller where nobody but mice was likely to discover them until spring. Then we began filling the bookcases with our exhibits.

Kids love collecting stuff, and enthusiasm amongst the club members reached fever pitch. During two successive weekends we laboriously hauled home scores of clay-coated bones from a landslip a mile away on the riverbank. I identified these as dinosaur bones. They may actually have belonged to buffalo, but more probably cows. We also scoured barns, back sheds, and attics in the neighborhood, from which we abstracted some rare and wonderful objects.

Until a few years ago I still had the "acquisition catalogue" in which was carefully inscribed a list of our exhibits. It has now gone from me but I remember some of the more interesting entries. There was, for instance, the joined skulls of a two-headed calf. There was an enormous umbrella stand made from the lower leg and foot of an elephant. And there was a gruesomely discolored human kidney in a jar of alcohol, "borrowed" from his doctor father by one of our members.

We also had a stand of mounted tropical birds which had originally been protected by a glass bell jar. The jar had since been broken and the birds had become home to legions of moths and a myriad of skin-bone-feather-eating little beetles called dermestids. The display had, in fact, become a sort of mini-menagerie whose enterprising members quickly colonized the professor's house.

Another prize possession was a decrepit stuffed black bear cub which had languished for too long in a damp basement. It stank with a peculiarly penetrating pungency.

It was our intention to hold a grand opening of the museum during the Christmas holidays. We planned to invite the mayor and other dignitaries. I had even written an announcement to be sent to the *Star Phoenix*, in which I extolled the uniqueness of our endeavor: "It is the most stupendous collection of natural and unnatural curiosities of all sexes ever gathered in Saskatoon."

Disaster struck before we could go public. The moths and beetles precipitated things by invading the cupboard where Helen kept her raccoon coat and establishing a lively colony there. And a week of wet weather brought the bear to such a peak of pungency that my parents finally got wind of what was happening below decks. Angus made an investigation which was immediately followed by an ultimatum. We were given twenty-four hours to disperse the Saskatchewan National Animal Museum or it would end up in the rubbish bin behind our house.

I was not entirely devastated by the loss of my museum. The collecting phase had come to an end in any case, and my tribe was losing interest. Moreover, I was already preparing to engage my little band in another enterprise.

In December of 1934 a new magazine joined the ranks of Canadian periodicals. As is the Canadian way, it did so without fanfare. *Nature Lore— The Official Organ of the Beaver Club of Amateur Naturalists* came quietly upon the scene. The cover portrayed a bloated sea-gull about to bomb a very shaggy beaver. The club's motto was inscribed below the beaver. *Natura Omnia Vincit* which, if my Latin is to be trusted, means Nature Conquers All.

The first issue contained: "*Stories and Articles and Poems About Animals, Birds and Reptiles, Together with Various Illustrations and Anecdotes by Members of the Club. Price 5 or 10 cents the Copy.*"

The variable asking price was, I submit, an act of genius. Those were Depression times so we dared not charge more than a nickel but, by giving the purchasers the option of paying ten cents in a good cause, we shamed most of them into doing just that.

It will come as no surprise to learn that Billy Mowat was the editor-in-chief. He wrote an impassioned editorial for the first issue, from which I quote:

"Birds and animals do not get heard enough in this country and are not treated well. The Beaver Club intends to do something about this. Every 5-cent bit contributed to this magazine will be spent on the betterment of the birds and animals of Saskatchewan..."

I also wrote most of the text, although I attributed many of the pieces to my loyal tribesfolk. It was the least I could do. They fanned out all over Saskatoon in fine weather and foul, hawking copies of the magazine to all and sundry.

The public's reception astounded us. Within a week the entire first issue, amounting to fifty copies, had sold out. The three subsequent issues, with press runs of a hundred copies each, did almost as well, earning a grand total of $25.45, which was more than many people were then being paid for a week's labor. This sum was almost pure profit because I had persuaded Angus to print *Nature Lore* on the library's mimeograph machine (using library ink and paper) as a charitable contribution to a worthy cause.

I believe it *was* worthy. The articles may have been a little didactic: "Planestrius migratorius [the robin] is a prominent local insectivor"; or somewhat overblown: "The crow can talk extremely well and is as intelligent as most people." Nevertheless, the effect was to at least engender some interest in and sympathy for wild creatures amongst people who had never previously given a thought to the possibility that they might have something in common with other animals.

As promised, we spent our money on good works. Each winter the discharge of hot water from the city's coal-fired electric generating plant maintained an open pond in the otherwise frozen river. This provided a haven for ducks and geese which were unable to join in the great southbound migration because of sickness or, more usually, because they had been wounded by hunters. In previous years, most of these unfortunates starved to death long before spring came, but during the winter of 1934-35 the Beaver Club saw to it that they were well-supplied with grain and corn. In so doing we set a precedent which, I understand, is still being followed by some of the worthy citizens of Saskatoon.

Enthusiasm for the Beaver Club waned sharply with the advent of warm weather. Most of the boys were infected with the spring craze for baseball and the girls with the spring craze for boys. Abandoned by most of its members, the club and *Nature Lore* quietly expired.

I was immune to the baseball virus and, since the testosterone coursing through my veins had not yet reached full flood, was more or less immune to girls as well. More or less. I sometimes had fantasies about Muriel Pinder, the dark-haired daughter of a druggist who had done exceedingly well for himself during the Prohibition years. Muriel lived in a rococo, strawberry-pink, stucco mansion a block away and was regarded by the boys of the neighborhood as hot stuff. Alas, she did not regard me in the same way. I wrote her a poem once.

> *No bird that flies in summer skies,*
> *No mouse that lurks in sacred church,*
> *No fish that swims in river dim,*
> *No snake that crawls on sunny walls*
> *Can stir my heart the way you do*
> *With raven hair and eyes so blue.*

She returned this offering by next day's post, with her critical evaluation written across it in purple ink.

"Ugh!"

Muriel may not have had a taste for me but her literary taste was impeccable.

And, I must now admit, that poem was not even truthful. Birds, mice, fish, snakes, indeed any creatures that lived in the wild were of more interest to me than any girl.

Although my parents generally approved of my activities, the zeal with which I was now pursuing my ornithological interests sometimes gave them pause.

Not content with trying to find out all I could about the external aspects of birds, I became interested in their internal machinery. Whenever I found a dead one that winter I would bring it home, thaw it out, and dissect it in the seclusion of my room. This could be a messy business, as on the occasion when the bird was an over-ripe prairie chicken. My mother attributed the consequent odor to "unwashed boy," and never knew what lurked for several days in an old pan under my bed.

My parents did, however, know about the woodpecker.

They were giving a dinner party one Sunday in January. It was a small, select party for adults only, very formal. The diners were having dessert when, in the midst of a solemn conversation about King George the Fifth's grave illness, I burst into the dining room, dancing with excitement, and bearing aloft a tin plate.

Since there was apparently nothing to be seen on the plate, Angus thought (or so he later said) I was playing Salome without the head. He had begun to reprove me for interrupting my elders, when I stopped him.

"Dad! Dad! I've *found* them! I've *got* them!"

One of the guests was Bessie Woodward, wife of the owner of Saskatoon's daily newspaper, the *Star Phoenix*. Now she asked politely, "Got what, Farley?"

"The testes of a hairy woodpecker! Just look!"

Whereupon I thrust my offering before her startled eyes. The testes were minute but I produced a magnifying glass so the guests could have a close look. Some people left their desserts unfinished.

Whatever Mrs. Woodward thought about it, her husband must have been intrigued. A week or so later he sent me a note asking if I would be interested in writing a weekly column about birds in the *Star*'s Saturday supplement for young people. This was a four-page tabloid called "Prairie Pals" which enjoyed a tremendous popularity with kids of all ages in those days before comic books.

The demise of *Nature Lore* had left me with no outlet for my writing so I seized upon this opportunity with an avidity which was not entirely untainted. Mr. Woodward had said I might be paid for my work if it proved acceptable.

I went all out. School work was neglected even more than usual. I wrote every day after school, picking with two fingers at my father's portable typewriter. I would have written every evening too but the sound of me clicking away apparently got to Angus and he reclaimed his typewriter after dinner to work on what he hoped might be a novel.

In mid-February I sent off a batch of four pieces then sat back to wait, alternating between gloom and hope. I heard nothing directly from the *Star* but when I opened "Prairie Pals" on the last day of the month, there I was in print, and this time in *real* print. The column was called "Birds of the Season" and an introductory paragraph by the editors informed all and sundry that it "came from the talented pen of young Farley Mowat of Saskatoon."

Now that I was formally launching myself into a career as a newspaper columnist, I had decided to come out of my Farley closet and give Billy the go-by, at least officially. The following week I got a check for four dollars—a dollar a column—and a note informing me that I would henceforth have a Thursday deadline to meet.

Heaven was here—was now! I flung myself on the typewriter, frantic to build up a backlog of columns in case I burned out and died young. Visions of achieving immortality as an author danced in my head. I pleaded with Angus to let me use his machine in the evenings and, delighted with his son's success, he agreed and his novel went into temporary abeyance.

Here is a sample from "Birds of the Season."

Snowy Owl
(Nyctea nyctea)

Gliding on silent wings over the unfathomable stillness of the frozen prairie, a great white bird floats eerily over the desolate bluffs and silent farms lying dark and shadowy below the shimmering Northern Lights. Across the bleak, snow-bound and wind-swept fields, a barely perceptible rabbit bounces with easy effort. As it passes over the unsuspecting hare the great shadow swerves and flits, moth-like, toward the ground. The unbroken silence is pierced by a quickly stifled scream and the shadowy folds of night envelop the last scene of the survival of the fittest.

…The Snowy Owl is one of the largest of the owl family…To the casual observer it appears as a large, earless, white bird, faintly streaked with brown and possessed of the most puzzlingly silent flight around which many fanciful tales are written. What little is known of the nesting of Nyctea seems to prove that it nests only in the Far North, laying its eggs in a hollow in the tundra. When they hatch, the Lemmings, Ptarmigan and other birds and mammals in the vicinity are sorely chivvied, for a young owl consumes enormous quantities of food before it becomes the hush-winged master of the tundra.

…Owls are not at all discriminating about what passes their rending beaks, and they swallow both the hair and the bones of their victims, including their skulls. When the digestive juices have taken all that is digestible the remains are regurgitated in a soggy ball. This is a wonderful provision of nature and might be a blessing to man if he could learn to do it too.

…The economic status of the Snowy Owl is on the useful side of the line. His food, while in our part of the country, is chiefly of small rodents and occasionally a sick or wounded Hungarian or Prairie Chicken. Hunters should not condemn him for this as he and all the other kinds of owls are only weeding out the unfit of the game birds, thereby leaving a better and healthier race to carry on.

When the Snowy leaves his wild retreat in the Far North do not welcome him here with shotguns and rifles and do not shoot him as vermin but let him live, a kingly bird among birds, fit to occupy the throne of Monarch of the Air.

This piece stirred up trouble. Angus came home from the library with a long face after being visited in his office by some of the local hunting fraternity, including prominent businessmen and a member of his own library board. They had made it clear that anybody who chose publicly to defend vermin against the interests of true sportsmen was pretty close to being vermin himself.

Angus told us about it over dinner.

"You know, Bunje, you could be wrong about the hawks and owls being so damned harmless. But you've got a perfect right to speak your mind about it *or* write about it. Don't let anyone ever tell you otherwise. Only…only for the love of God *do* stay away from birth control or anti-temperance league propaganda in future columns."

This was followed by a good-natured word from Mr. Woodward when next I saw him. "Best not write about hunters any more, Billy," he warned me. "They're a touchy lot."

I played it cool in my next few columns. However, when the first twinges of spring began making themselves felt, I got carried away.

I wrote a piece about the Ruddy Duck in which I devoted a long paragraph to an enthusiastic and graphic description of how this agile little bird makes love under water.

Angus had not thought to warn me to leave sex out of my writing. I'm sure he wished he had because when my column reached the editorial office of the *Star* all hell broke loose. Someone—we were never told who—passed it on to someone else in a women's church league, and the fat was in the fire.

Angus and Helen got several letters accusing them of unforgivable laxity in dealing with my religious education and in allowing me to become contaminated by the evils of sex. "This child," wrote one good lady, "will go straight to hell unless he is led back into the paths of clean thought and Godly behavior. If he is sent to burn forever, it will be your fault!"

Indignation against my piece flared up so rapidly and fiercely that the *Star Phoenix* bowed before it. With some embarrassment, Mr. Woodward showed Angus a letter from a local businessman who threatened to withhold advertising from the paper "if you allow such disgusting prurience to be placed before the eyes of our children." I believe Mr. Woodward was sorry about what he had to do. He at least saw to it that I was paid for the piece that never ran; but no more "Birds of the Season" appeared in "Prairie Pals."

The Young Writer

Less than ten years later, Mowat was serving in Italy in the Second World War. During that time, he and his parents exchanged many letters. He also sent home some of the writing he was attempting. The following selections from much longer letters show his father's encouragement and his own strengthening resolve to become a writer.

Dear Friend Squibb (Mark II).—

It used to be "Squib" when I had it alone but as you insist on adding the redundant "b" I'll follow suit.

Last Monday was a big day in Kingston. Helen got two airmails and two airgraphs from you, but the latest dated more than a month ago. There was also a package containing a chapter of Mutt and two pages of verse.* The chapter about old Mutt and the skunks is the best you've done yet but, damn it, didn't I say not to use that story? Didn't I say I had already written it and offered it to a publisher—and had it refused? Is it any wonder nobody makes you a captain when you can't even obey the simplest order?

Although your letters take an age to reach us, you are a good lad about writing. Did you guess that a couple of us do not live for much else? Which puts a rather unfair burden upon your shoulders, but I don't very well see how it can be helped.

You send us your verses, and I am grateful and then I don't know what to do about it. You say: "They are just dashed off, you can doctor them up," or words to that effect. So I read them again and again and I sit staring out the window and don't know what to do. I wish dear old Mutt was here— *he'd* know.

In the first place, I am neither a poet nor a qualified critic. In the second place, to tamper with the fruits of another man's meditations is little short of a sin against the Holy Ghost. In the third place, I can't do it objectively, as I might if you were here. But you aren't here. And we can't see you objectively any more because you are too far away, and too much in my thoughts, and the emotional strain of waiting for an official telegram about you is too great.

I must now confess that I sent three of your poems to *The Atlantic*. They haven't come back yet, but they will. And I'll send 'em somewhere else. Nothing like starting at the top.

---

* Over the war years, I sent home a number of sketches about Mutt, the dog of my youth, which were eventually incorporated into *The Dog Who Wouldn't Be* (1957).

[San Leonardo, Ortona Front]

Jan 11

Dear Ma, and the Other Squib:

Got two hundred cigarettes from you but have received no parcels for a long time. But then neither has anyone else. Chapter 7 of *It's a Dog's Life* is now ready for the presses. Gets worse and worse, but I have fun pounding it out between bangs.

[Ottawa]

Feb 22

Dear Mark II.—

Here's a surprise. Reg Saunders* insists on seeing what you've sent me of *The Dog*. He is also so anxious to get at *Carrying Place* that he is even going to have

---

* A publisher who had expressed interest in publishing *Carrying Place*, Angus Mowat's novel.

169

his stenographer type a clean manuscript from my much-written-over copy. I read it straight through to my best critic over the weekend. I don't know what I'd do without my best critic. I ask her to criticize. She criticizes. I get mad. And, damn it all, the woman has been right every time so far, and probably always will be right. That's what makes me mad.

Your Momma has great hopes for you as a writer. She says you write so much better than I did at your age. Easy, since I didn't write at all then. And besides, she says, you are already more mature than I'll ever be. Something in that, joking aside. I'll always be so damned unsophisticated, as a writer I mean. But, oh gosh, if it could only come down to two of us pecking at two typewriters in two cabins at two ends of some little island like Waupoos, or down where the Black River flows into South Bay....

[Ottawa]

Feb 25

Well, *The Dog's Life* and *Carrying Place* are both on their way to Reg Saunders. It's a hell of a state of affairs when a man's son gets to compete with him in the open market like that.

Anyhoo, you just keep on pecking and pecking at the mayor of Assoro's typewriter.* It's practice and practice that does it. And there is likely to be a great writers' market after this war. And with that, and your interest in birds, you can live a pretty ideal kind of life. If you have read much about writers, which I know you have NOT (repeat), you will realize that in a great number of cases it has taken two generations to make the best of them. The old man starts, but remains a plodding minor, and then the son comes along and becomes noted. Now that would suit me very well indeed. I'll go on plodding.

---

* An Olivetti portable "liberated" from the mayor's office in the Sicilian village of Assoro. It was my constant companion until war's end.

[Kingston]

Mar 5

Dear Farl.—

I am sorry to say that *Atlantic*, very politely and with a nice letter in which they asked me to write and thank you, hasn't taken your verse. I'll try somebody else.

[Kingston]

Mar 13

My Dear Son.—

I sent some of your verses to Reg, who replied: "Dear Angus: The poems of Farley's are first class but we need more to make a book. If we can get enough I would not hesitate one moment to publish." But the hell of it is I sent him the best and the others aren't as good but I'll send them anyway. My son, don't let your writing go, no matter what happens.

[Ortona]

Mar 9

Dear Folks:

The mails are in! And what a haul—several from you two, all of fairly recent date. Some things you say leave me puzzled. What the hell's all this about waiting to hear from *Atlantic Monthly?* Have you been peddling my letters to the illiterate populace again? Or are you serializing *Carrying Place?* Explain yourself, Poppa.

Sent a cable yesterday. Seems like it might be a good idea to send a couple every month, if your nerves are equal to the strain. Letters get sunk or crash en route, but cables go so deep the U-boats canna get them!

I'm delighted *Carrying Place* is finally finished. I was afraid its skipper had scuttled it long ago. I'm sure it will do better than *Then I'll Look Up.** It better had: going to be tough for the three of us to live on Pop's First War pension without something coming in on the side. Speaking of which: your comments on the possibility of me earning a pleasant, if scanty, living by birding and writing is prescient. I had decided to do just that some time ago. According to Mum, I've saved something like two thousand from my pay in the past two years, which isn't bad for a Mowat. Together with my little legacy from Aunt Lillian, I should be able to get by on what I've got for a couple of years.

And what's this about letting Reg Saunders look at the *Dog's Life?* That is high school stuff! For the Lord's sake, take it away from him. I may *want* him to publish a book some day and don't want him turned off too soon. The stuff I am writing here is purely for my own recreation and I send it along just for your amusement. It ain't possible to write for publication under these circumstances.

[Ortona]

Mar 2

Dear Folks:

An hour ago I returned from an eight-day leave in the southern city of Bari, which is now an 8th Army leave center and, as any map will tell you, a good-ish way from the war.

And, yes, I had the Mayor's typewriter rebuilt by its manufacturer whilst in Bari. They offered to buy it back for a king's ransom (they can't manufacture any new ones) but I wouldn't play. It is the living symbol of my ongoing existence, you might say, even though I've given up on the *Dog's Life*. The effort of trying to be funny just takes too much out of me these days, and most of

---

* Angus's first novel, published in 1936.

what I write isn't funny anyway—just flip. Maybe I'll go back to it sometime. Meanwhile I'm still writing terrible, terrible poetry, just to keep in practice.

[Ortona]

April 1

Dear Squib and Consort:

The Mayor's typewriter is ribbonless tonight so you'll have to put up with my hieroglyphs.

Drafted the last chapter of the Mutt book last week, so now I can be rid of the damn thing. I'll send it back by surface package and if it doesn't make it past the U-boats, no great loss. It has served its purpose by helping me get a grip on myself.

I'm going to lay off writing poetry. The stuff is getting so damned morose that it gives even me the creeps.

[north of Naples]

May 8

During the current period of relative inaction, I've indulged in some introspection and realize, to my surprise, that I've done a lot of maturing recently. That isn't a very profound discovery, but a bit of a shock to a perennial juvenile. I find I'm a lot more tolerant, because I have to be. And lazier, and less ambitious. And I'm not prepared to submerge the pleasure-giving aspects, if any, of whatever lies ahead in an eternally receding vista of a rosy future that demands incessant labor. I figure now that the whole work ethic is a con man's trick being played on us by the same lot who stand to make a bundle from the war. On the other hand, I don't want to be a lotus eater. I like to work— at what I like to work at; bird studies maybe, or writing, but not for the money in it, or so I can die rich. I've spent much of the best (or at least the best so far) years of my life doing things I hate; living a way of life that I detest;

173

forfeiting all the things that really pleasured me. So I'm going to live the first few years after it's over *my* way; doing what *I* want to do; even if I have to starve ten years from now in consequence. I can't make up for the years of war without some cost, and if I have to mortgage my long-term future, then so be it.

I am beginning to think my future is going to be in the north. The *Far North*, or, as old Stefansson used to say, "the friendly Arctic." So I want to get away from it all? Yep, that's exactly what I want.

[Toronto]

May 12

Dear Squibbles.—

I see I haven't written to you since May 1. This continual flitting about the country inspecting libraries that I am now engaged in upsets normal schedules.

Hell, that wasn't any veiled comment about the *Atlantic Monthly*. One of my letters must have gone astray. I wonder how many have done that. Anyway, you'll know by now that they didn't want your verse.

[Toronto]

Oct 13

Dear Mk II.—

Frank Hammond has finally sent along the package of papers you gave him to bring home to us and we have read and re-read them with what avidity you may guess. I am fascinated by the battle narratives and stories. "Stephen Bates"* is far and away the best thing you have ever done. If a publisher doesn't take that, then they are crazy.

---

* A story sent with a letter home.

Squibbie boy, you must fight like hell not to let malaria, the army, frustration or anything else get you down because you were born to write, and you've got to keep level-headed to write even though you may write the most un-level-headed things at times. Which we all do if we start young enough. Which was my great mistake, that I didn't. Damn it. Now here's a funny thing. In your verse you dip down into the depths and fling restraint to the winds and come out with things that are pretty much like "Strange Fruit" but lack conviction because, I think, they do lack restraint. But in your prose you get disciplined, and all first-class writing is closely disciplined. *Grapes of Wrath*, which is a masterpiece, is one of the most disciplined books I've ever read, and one of the most powerful. Why you should miss it in your verse and catch it in your prose is puzzling. My guess is that the verse is practice for the prose, although you may not see it that way at all.

So long, old feller. Keep a steady hand.

[near Riccione]

Oct

This is a business letter. Simple and straightforward.

Send me, please, the following: *Pocket Oxford English Dictionary*; Fowler's *Modern English Usage*; *Roget's Thesaurus*; six of Mr. Remington's portable ribbons; an anthology of Conrad's best stories, and some sort of punctuation guide that will enable me to tell when not to use a semi-colon. Kindly oblige at the earliest instant or, as we say in the Ahmy, deal with soonest.

What's up? My back is, and if I have to go on floundering in this witch's cauldron I'm going to try to turn it to my own account. In short, I'm going to write and write like hell, not for publication, or future fame or peltry, but to keep myself afloat. I may not succeed, but I'll bust a gut trying.

[Richmond Hill]

Nov 22

Dear Squibbles.—(All right—two b's)

Well, I finally got two of your war stories typed out in readable form and added a few commas (and took out about three thousand unnecessary ones) and, on my way to *Maclean's* magazine, let Reg see them. He says they are too strong for *Maclean's* but he is going to talk it over with Napier Moore, the big shot of that rag. What Reg really wants to do, and I can see him edging around to it, is to make up a little volume of your stories and verse. However, it would be too slight as yet.

The great thing, of course, for anybody who aspires to write, is to get into print. Stimulus. It seems to engender a sense of responsibility. You feel that you aren't talking to a brick wall any more and, having been in print once, you simply *must* do it again and keep on doing it. Nobody amounted to anything, or very few did, till they began to achieve some kind of volume. Not that one should sell his birthright for volume; that would, naturally, be fatal.

Anyhoo, I'm busting to see you in print as soon as possible. You've got the knack and the flair for it, and you are so young that if you got started now you'd have a long writing life ahead of you, trench mortars and shell-fire permitting. And that is very important. I got started much too late—in everything except getting married and having a brat.

[Miramare]

Dec 2

Dear Folks:
No sign of the writing books. Please repeat the order. If both lots should arrive, I have a pal who also thinks he wants to be a writer. As for the publication of "my war stories," don't bother trying. In fact, *don't* try. After reading your last letter, I read them over and was appalled by my inept treatment of things I had thought I felt deeply enough about to describe accurately. Maybe I

should go back to writing Fourth Form essays for Miss Izaard at Richmond Hill High.

[Toronto]

Dec 6

Dear Cap.—

I am chuckling with glee at a resounding joke that has befallen my son. You will remember him—little Farley Mowat who used to live in Saskatoon and edited a mimeographed magazine called *Nature Lore* that had a column headed "Little Bitch of Laughter"? Well, some time ago my son sent me three terrible attempts at storytelling, but the one called "Stephen Bates" was accepted by *Maclean's* magazine and should appear in about six weeks.

Now here's where the joke comes in. Mr. Maclean goes to Defence HQ and can't get permission to publish the story under my son's own name. This joke can be made to backfire, however. Mr. Maclean and I shall just invent a pseudonym (look that up in your new dictionary, which I assume you have got by now). Something like "Pink Skunk" or "Low Lifer."

But the real joke about it all is that under army regulations, a member of the Canadian Army (Active) cannot accept remuneration for *any*thing. This is done so he will not get rich and forget about fighting a war. You see the joke?

However, even this can be made to turn around. Mr. Maclean is going to pay *me* the money. It's one hundred bucks. Just think of that! One hundred berries for a little short story, when I only stand to clear five hundred for a full-length novel that wins wide acclaim and takes two years to perpetrate. So this part of the joke is on me, or would be, except for the fact that *I* get the dough for your story.

But hark ye. Even as I wrote that last line I began to see another side to the joke. *I'll have to pay income tax on your damn money.*

So, in the end the joke's on all of us.

And I had to submit to letting Mr. Maclean take out most of the "damns" and all the "bastards" and "sons of bitches." He says his great journal is for the home, not the barrack room. Maybe you'll forgive me. The piece bleeds a bit with the language purged, but the great thing is you've got your start. Just keep on hewing at that block of wood you call your head and my prophecy about the Remington (typewriter) in the bow of the canoe will come to pass.

Your mother and I are more thrilled than we have been about my two books combined. If you come through this war, son, you can make yourself free! FREE—got that? You may be free to semi-starve, but you'll be free to live. Gosh, how I am excited!

So *au revoir, competitor.*

[Toronto]

Dec 9

Dear Farl.—

A brief note in haste. It's not "Stephen Bates," but "Liaison Officer" that *Maclean's* will publish. Apparently the bitterness in the Bates story, which was not your bitterness but that of many thousands of fighting men, is not considered to be conducive to Canadian Unity and to the War Effort. This is your first experience of censorship of literary people by the Establishment. Please take note that it will not be your last, although it will probably not be called by that name once the war is over.

[Toronto]

Dec 28

Dear Captain Mowat.—

Today at lunch time I went down to Ashbridge's to look at your boat. There she sat with two feet of snow on her deck and frozen in as snug as you please. And hardly a drop of water in her bilges.

So I take your writing too seriously? Nuts to you, feller. I didn't say, did I, that you are a Thomas Hardy or an Anthony Trollope or even a Mr. Tolstoi? I only said that, bar getting yourself killed by a stinking mortar bomb or shell, you can plan for a life after this hellish business is over, based on something you can do. I understand full well that the *Maclean's* acceptance, which your mother and I considered terrific news, would appear to a fellow going into action for the Nth time about as relevant as the price of eggs in Rosthern, Saskatchewan.

[Bagnacavallo]

Jan 4, 1945

Dear Parents:

My heart rejoices! The box of writer's aids has at long last arrived. Visitors to my stone crypt in the casa Brigade HQ presently occupies are at last showing a decent respect for the cloak-and-dagger boys, as we I-blokes are called,

usually with ridicule intended. When they look at my bookshelf and its shining new contents, they now salaam reverently and swallow their usual lewd jests. A dictionary! A thesaurus! A punctilious punctuation manual! *And* Fowler's *Modern English Usage*! These provide a formidable demonstration of our right to be deemed Intelligent. Whether or not or for what purposes we use said intelligence is, of course, a horse of a different texture. But I've already discovered how to spell sucess—or is it succes? I doubt it.

[in reserve at Cesenatico on the Coast]

Feb. 15

Dear Folks:

I've written, and torn up, a couple of short stories. They served a purpose, if only to demonstrate that I will likely not be in a mental condition to write a good story of any sort until some years after the pax.

I continue planning the cabana I will one day build on the northern fiords of B.C. and will soon send a sheaf of draftings of same. I figure that living on my capital (a shudder goes through the whole capitalist world) I can exist for at least five years, and by then my typewriter ought to be earning me sufficient pennies to go on with which.

It's amazing, the strength of this urge to retreat to one of Nature's hideouts. You did it in your time—fire-ranging in the Nipigon. Do you think it might be the same instinct that sends wounded animals into hiding looking for healing?

[Oostmalle]

March 23

Dear Folks:

You express a certain wonderment about my lack of interest in the story in *Maclean's*. Well, I'll tell you. It stinks, my fond parents, and you and I all know it does, but you won't say so. However, that isn't the trouble. The trouble is that I can't either fix that story or write anything new. I've tried like blazes to write, just for the reassurance that putting words on paper gives me. But after a para or two, my interest just can't be flogged into further action. I haven't quit trying but I figure I might as well.

[Ouderkerk]

June 24

Your self-reliant offspring who usually scorns advice is in need of some of same.

I am getting scared.

It is now the second month since the war ended, taking with it my excuse for carting around an empty skull. It is time that I snapped out of it. But I can't seem to "snap."

I sit down to write. I believe I *can* write. A paragraph or so of reasonably good descriptive material comes out without much trouble. I stare at it. But no more comes. No *story* comes. In fury I rip the paper up and go down to one of our workshops and spend the rest of the afternoon, or evening, stripping down some piece of German military wizardry to see what makes it work. I'd rather dice with a deadly device that might blow up in my face than stare at the hateful machine upon which I cannot write.

But the writing block is not the worst. The worst is that I am turning more and more to total immersion in purely mechanical activities. This seems to be becoming all that I can will myself to do. Now what in the hell does that mean? There is no real satisfaction in it—just a means to pass the time away. Although I suppose it is better than passing time with the bottle, it still leads nowhere. I have to flog my interest even to keep this war museum caper going and perhaps *delude* myself that I am doing something worthwhile. And it all boils down to this: the only certainty I have is that I *can still find ways to pass the time*. A conclusion that cheers me up no end.

Where, for Chrissake, is the *purpose?*

So I ask you, Pop, how did you get into the swing of living once again?

So much for this *cri de coeur*. If I don't cool down I'm going to have liver troubles in my old age. If there is an old age.

[Toronto]

July 4

Dear Bothered and Bewildered.—

I have two thoughts to offer. The first for your comfort and the second for your enlightenment. The one is that you are several jumps ahead of where your old man was twenty-five years ago, because you do realize the trouble, and I didn't. I was just miserable and "lazy" and headed for life in the back alley without the vaguest notion of what was wrong. If I had had the wit to see that, I should have pulled myself out of it a lot sooner. It's a bad sickness. But at least you have diagnosed it, and the fact that you are worried is a most encouraging sign. To be frank, I was preparing myself to go into all this with you on your return. I didn't expect it to happen so soon. But it has. So, good.

Then, for your enlightenment, you've got an inherited characteristic which is going to make it harder for you, and which you will probably never overcome. Not that you ought to. You are sporadic. So's your old man. So was my old man. I have never worked steadily, ploddingly at anything in my life and neither will you. We push our efforts at great speed for a time, really concentrating, then we've simply got to drop it for another time and do something else. That may be reprehensible in the eyes of some but it is the way I am, and I've seen it in you, son, so many times I have come to take it for granted.

I hardly think you'd like to settle down and throw yourself with enthusiasm into the business of selling life insurance, for instance. Certainly not. You can't go about half-listening to birds in the woods, or half-dreaming as you dig an acre of spuds, or half-nothing as you splice a lot of rope, or doing other unnecessary things—not and sell insurance.

Now I know I am absolutely right in all the above, so starting from that basis, we have to figure out where you go from here. First, you can't go anywhere until you are out of the army, and out of it long enough to get quit of *that particular* soporific influence. You have to get *cured* of the army, and I use the word advisedly. Like both your parents, you are particularly sensitive to atmosphere and, like them, you absorb and hatch ideas rather than think them out the hard way. Whether you can write now or can't write now, whether you want to write now or want to potter about with bombs, these things don't matter a hoot. There's got to be a transition period of rest and cure.

The second step I am most positive about. Perhaps I oughtn't to mention it until you are cured of the army, but I will anyhow and you can put it out of mind till later if you want to. This is the matter of the new discipline which will have to supplant the army discipline. Face it. Not even people of our temperament can do without discipline. We may even need it more than most. And we've got to impose it on ourselves if we aren't going to spend all our lives digging blindly in the soil, or quite aimlessly whistling in the dark woods. That's what your trouble is right now. You are abandoning the army discipline, and you've never had any other kind inside yourself because when you enlisted you were still too young to have need of it. Also, you still had parental discipline, such as that was.

I am speaking very earnestly from my own experience when I say that the best way I know to encourage and develop this state is through a few years at university. Now don't howl! Forget about it if you want to but I am going to be insistent when the time comes. Speaking from experience? And how! Would I go back to college in 1918? Would I, hell! I used to become profanely contemptuous at the very thought. My mistake, brother. If it hadn't been for the influence of your mother (and the insults of *my* mother), I should never have made the first, tentative steps in that direction.

But it was the best thing I ever did for my mind. Mental discipline made easy. Directed reading. The discipline lay in the direction and in the assignments that came out of it. That's the outside discipline. But the inside discipline, the solid strata upon which I have lived my very happy life ever since, was the reading itself. The exposure of my little mind to the whole mind of the race and all its experiences.

That's the answer, son, for the man of temperament who wants to live fully—not just make a living—and, most emphatically, it is the answer for the man who finds life interesting enough so that he feels the need to write about it himself. Which you have the gift to do, and which I firmly believe you will do, never mind your present illness.

Against my insistence in this matter you will say, as I said, that it's too late, and that you've lost enough time as it is. You will point out that many of your peers have already settled down to sell life insurance while those who thoughtfully stayed home from the war and went to college instead have already graduated. O.K. They'll all be four or five years ahead of you. So what? Everything you were born to do can't be done at its best till maturity, anyway.

You've got everything in hand for the living of a very full (and probably impecunious) life, feller—except the two things I've been talking about. Civilian discipline, and sufficient of the background of your race, or tribe, or species, or whatever you choose to call it. Three or four years of college should suffice to meet this lack whether or not you bother to get a degree....

I trust you won't be hurt but the truth is that you are not one of the ones I am really worried about, although I do ache for you. And I am so deeply gratified that you should write to me as you did.

[Toronto]

July 12

I am to advise you that you are now a contributor to *Saturday Night*. When *Maclean's* admitted that "In Amsterdam There Lived a Man," "Last Days of Bremen" and "Dear Diary" were too good for it, I promptly sent them off to *Sat. Night*, and got only one back. And a personal letter from the editor, B. K. Sandwell, who (as you probably did not know) is one of the literary figures in this country, in which he says: "Your son in Holland certainly wields an extremely dexterous pen. I am delighted to have the two sketches, one about the distillery and the other about Amsterdam. I am returning herewith 'Dear Diary' which is not so effective."

And scribbled in his own handwriting: "They are really awfully good stuff."

So Pop's chirping like the veritable herd of robins and grackles that have descended on the cherry tree and stripped it. I mean to say that, while you are still not a Conrad, or a Hardy, or a Steinbeck, there is hope that all may not be lost. And I gather to my breast with even greater assurance the main dream of my life, which is that my son will one day write *the* book (and get $500 for it probably), which I think I shall never accomplish. Not, mind you, that I don't write good books—but not *the* one.

What a pity that you have no academic education. Wot a pity!

[Ouderkerk]

July 5

Dear Parents:

Stop worrying about my return. I'm alive and well.

I'm not doing any writing, little thinking and less talking. But I'm happy enough, and I think I shall be able to rehabilitate satisfactorily when I have to—which is not yet.

[Richmond Hill]

Aug 28

Dearest Bunje.

Get a move on and come home.

Your story about Bremen came out in *Saturday Night* last week, and I hope you'll soon get into your stride and continue to write as you certainly have the gift, doing it so easily. You were always a reasonable child so you must see it is time you gave up the flesh-pots of Belgium for the writer's proverbial life in a garret in Richmond Hill. Angus's scheme now is to buy four acres in the country and farm and keep bees.

[Richmond Hill]

Sept 7

Darling Bunje.

Sat. Night lies before me with your second story in it and I'd think you'd be thrilled about it. Angus is very disappointed that you don't seem to care, when he is so proud of your writing.

[Oostmalle]

Sept 23

Dear Folks:

This letter may be premature but I'll take the chance.

What I think is, that after five months of floundering about, the currents have at last carried me far enough inshore so that I can touch bottom and still keep my head above water. I begin to feel *normal*, or at least as normal as I can ever hope to feel.

As an indication of the above, I've finished the first draft of a five-thousand-word short story—a story I've been thinking about for the past couple of years and simply couldn't write. I did it this time in just four days of totally concentrated work.

It isn't much good but that isn't the point. The point being that I did it at all, and that I can again focus my interest on something and keep it focused until the job is done. *C'est bon*, eh?

I may suffer a relapse from this current state of well-being, but it won't be permanent, as I was beginning to feel my lengthy period of mental and spiritual despondency was becoming. So I feel "Ver goot!" as Bob Jespers, our tame town mayor, is fond of saying....

[Oostmalle]

Oct 18

The story I told you about has now gone into the stove. Not surprising, since it was really pretty bad. But not to worry: I was and am pleased that I wrote it at all, even though both plot and treatment weren't worth keeping. I am, in fact, much strengthened in the resolve to write for a living.

[Toronto]

Oct 31

Dear Almost Major Mk II.—

Yours of the eighteenth is just at hand and so interesting I have to reply at once. Mum says she told me so and you'll be home for Christmas but I still remain skeptical.

You are a damned young fool to write a story and then burn it. I never burned a story that I had finished. I might lay it away in lavender with the tear stains as memories, but burn it? Never! It is improvident. You never know when you might pick it out of the files and re-write it in satisfactory form. And anyway, everything you write is a product of the subconscious and is going to crop up again, as sure as hell.

[Antwerp]

Oct 26

Dear Parents:

This may or may not arrive before I do. If it does, then you can expect your wandering son to follow closely on its heels.

⊳━◆━○━◆━⊲

Angus was a very persuasive man. After I was discharged, he persuaded me to enroll at the University of Toronto, but the academic scene was unable to hold me long and by 1947 I had been seduced by the Arctic and was beginning the writer's life which I have followed ever since.

Angus never published another book. He and Helen remained together until, at the age of seventy-two, he abandoned my mother for a lady librarian thirty-three years his junior. Although he never returned to Helen, she bore him no grudge. Whether he ever forgave himself is another matter.

During his final years, relations between him and me grew strained, partly because of my feelings about his treatment of my mother, and partly because he began to disapprove of my work on the stated grounds that I had betrayed my talent by writing nonfiction instead of novels. Since he had heretofore expressed much pride in my work, I was hurt and resentful and, consequently, did less than I might have done to heal the differences which were dividing us one from the other.

When he died in 1977 at the age of eighty-four years, I mourned his passing as a son mourns a father, and perhaps that is how things would have remained had I not found myself (or been led?) back into another time by re-reading and re-living the letters he wrote to me during the war.

Now I mourn him in a different way: as a loving friend whose steadfastness and infinite understanding helped me to endure and to survive the roughest years of my life.

Books by Farley Mowat

People of the Deer	1952
The Regiment	1955
Lost in the Barrens	1956
The Dog Who Wouldn't Be	1957
The Grey Seas Under	1958
Coppermine Journey	1958
The Desperate People	1959
Ordeal by Ice	1960
Owls in the Family	1961
The Serpent's Coil	1961
The Black Joke	1962
Never Cry Wolf	1963
Westviking	1965
The Curse of the Viking Grave	1966
Canada North	1967
The Polar Passion	1967
This Rock Within the Sea	1968
The Boat Who Wouldn't Float	1969
Sibir	1970
A Whale for the Killing	1972
Tundra	1973
Wake of the Great Sealers	1973
The Snow Walker	1975
Canada North Now	1976
And No Birds Sang	1979
The World of Farley Mowat (Peter Davison, ed.)	1980
Sea of Slaughter	1984
My Discovery of America	1985
Virunga	1987
The New Founde Land	1989
Rescue the Earth	1990
My Father's Son	1992
Born Naked	1993
Aftermath	1995

Acknowledgments

All the pieces in this book were selected from books that Farley Mowat has had published over his forty-five-year career. The following is a chapter-by-chapter breakdown, which will help you find the books themselves so you can continue to discover the world of Farley Mowat.

The Family Mowat

"Beginnings," "A Note About Names," "Angus and Boats," and "Moving West" are all excerpted from Farley Mowat's autobiography, *Born Naked*, published in 1993 by Key Porter Books in Canada and Houghton Mifflin in the United States. Reprinted here with the permission of the publishers and the author.

Mutt

"The Coming of Mutt," "Mutt's Early Days," "Battle Tactics," "Vignettes of Travel," and "April Passage" are pieces taken from one of Mowat's best-loved books, *The Dog Who Wouldn't Be*, first published in 1957 and reprinted here by arrangement with Little, Brown and Company and McClelland and Stewart Limited and with the kind permission of the author. "Mutt Goes Hunting" is comprised of excerpts from *Born Naked* and *The Dog Who Wouldn't Be*.

The Others

"Discovering the Others" and "Saskatoon, 1935" are taken from *Born Naked*. "Wol and Weeps" is a small part of Mowat's tale of his owl companions that is called *Owls in the Family*, first published in 1961 and reprinted here by arrangement with Little, Brown and Company and McClelland and Stewart Limited and with the kind permission of the author. "The Family Lupine" is from *Never Cry Wolf*, first published in 1963 and reprinted here by arrangement with Little, Brown and Company and McClelland and Stewart Limited and with the kind permission of the author. "The Whale" is an excerpt from

A Whale for the Killing, first published in 1972 and reprinted here by arrangement with Little, Brown and Company and McClelland and Stewart Limited and with the kind permission of the author. "Peter and the Birds" appears in *Aftermath: Travels in a Post-War World*, published in 1995 by Key Porter Books in Canada and by Roberts Rinehart in the United States. Reprinted here by permission of the publishers and the author.

Adventures

"On the Water" is from *The Dog Who Wouldn't Be*. "In the Arctic" can be found in *Born Naked*. "On the Salt Seas" is taken from Mowat's classic *The Boat Who Wouldn't Float*, first published in 1969 and reprinted here by arrangement with Little, Brown and Company and McClelland and Stewart Limited and with the kind permission of the author.

Becoming a Writer

The selections in "The Young Naturalist" are taken from *Born Naked*. "The Young Writer" section is made up of letters contained in Mowat's war memoir *My Father's Son*, published in 1992 by Key Porter Books in Canada and Houghton Mifflin in the United States. Reprinted here by permission of the publishers and the author.